Loneliness

A Practical Guide For Improving Your Self-esteem

(How To Deal With And Overcome Loneliness To Never Feel Alone Again)

Joseph Beale

Published By **Tyson Maxwell**

Joseph Beale

All Rights Reserved

Loneliness: A Practical Guide For Improving Your Self-esteem (How To Deal With And Overcome Loneliness To Never Feel Alone Again)

ISBN 978-1-77485-644-4

All rights reserved. No part of this guidebook shall be reproduced in any form without permission in writing from the publisher except in the case of brief quotations embodied in critical articles or reviews.

Legal & Disclaimer

The information contained in this ebook is not designed to replace or take the place of any form of medicine or professional medical advice. The information in this ebook has been provided for educational & entertainment purposes only.

The information contained in this book has been compiled from sources deemed reliable, and it is accurate to the best of the Author's knowledge; however, the Author cannot guarantee its accuracy and validity and cannot be held liable for any errors or omissions. Changes are periodically made to this book. You must consult your doctor or get professional medical advice before using any of the suggested remedies, techniques, or information in this book.

Upon using the information contained in this book, you agree to hold harmless the Author from and against any damages, costs, and expenses, including any legal fees potentially resulting from the application of any of the information provided by this guide. This disclaimer applies to any damages or injury caused by the use and application, whether directly or indirectly, of any advice or information presented, whether for breach of contract, tort, negligence, personal injury, criminal intent, or under any other cause of action.

You agree to accept all risks of using the information presented inside this book. You need to consult a professional medical practitioner in order to ensure you are both able and healthy enough to participate in this program.

TABLE OF CONTENTS

Chapter 1 Loneliness Is A Problem ...1

Chapter 2 The Stages Of Loneliness..9

Chapter 3 Feeling Shy 30

Chapter 4 Communication Improvement...................................51

Chapter 5 Young And Lonely 77

Chapter 6 The Middle Years And Loneliness..93

Chapter 1 Loneliness is a Problem

Nearly everyone feels lonely from time to time. Many of us feel isolated most of all. Different surveys have shown that more than half of single adults feel lonely and almost a quarter are married. Some people have been feeling lonely for as long and will continue to feel this way throughout their entire lives. Some suffer from extreme loneliness and know it will end in weeks or even months. All ages are affected----children, adolescents, young men and women, the middle-aged and the elderly.

Lonely persons are people who feel isolated. They need someone to talk to and establish a special relationship. Certain things are needed to keep a special relationship alive once it has been formed.

A good relationship involves both of you sharing the important events that happen in your life.

It is through communication that people can share things. This is how people can experience, understand, respond, and share what other people feel. Communication between two people is perfect. When they are sharing the same experiences, they can each be fully aware of how they react to one another. Communication is essential to building strong relationships. How does communication go well?

Communication works because communication relies on a few very specific human behaviors. These behaviours are speaking, listening, touching, feeling, and looking. You can experience each of these behaviours in three different ways. You can also impose them on someone else. One example is that we can talk with another person, no matter if he or she is listening. Another example is that we can touch another person near us. So, when it comes to talking, listening and touching another person, we can be the passive person. We could also be passive and are listened to or touched. If someone is talking at you, it is obvious that no communication can occur if we are not actively involved.

We listen to the noise that he makes and are not affected by his meaning. We know that he's trying to send a message. But, we refuse to believe it. We remain detached and uninvolved. It is possible to be very passive about someone listening in to a conversation between us and another person. Being touched or looked at by another person can make us passive.

Each communication behavior can be used for a third purpose. This is where the action of talking and listening are combined.

Touching and looking are mutual. A couple may talk to, listen, touch, or look at their partner.

These four behaviors are mutually beneficial when people are communicating well. It is not impossible for one person to do the same thing as the other. You are not more active or passive than your partner. They are perfect together. They are equals, both valuable, and that shows. They know each other well and don't want to be separated.

Even in the best relationships, there is no perfect communication. For proof, you only have to watch happy couples for a couple of minutes. Each one will be slightly more active or less passive than their partner. For example, one may reach out and touch the hands of the other.

But, the touch is most often received actively, not passively.

Good communication requires a lot of mutual behaviours. The most important thing is that mutual actions show that people care and how much they care. The more there is mutual behavior, the greater our knowledge that the other person cares. The less mutual behaviour we have, the more we know that he/she cares.

Communication is important because it gives us information about how valuable our actions are to another person. It also allows us give the person information about how important we think he/she is. Our self-worth is measured by what we receive from other people. It's important that people feel comfortable around us and trust us. If we truly matter to someone, our communication skills will allow us to share rewards and get rewards in a more or less equal manner. Without trusting others, we are unable to take on the risk of expressing our true feelings. We keep some things to ourselves and are more passively or actively hostile towards others. We either reject some of our own, or we accept part of the other individual, or both.

Talking to others helps you to see your own value. But it also helps you to see the value in the world around us. When we can't assess these values due to having no one to talk with, we feel lonely. We are starved to death of mutual behaviours. It is therefore quite different than those periods when people withdraw from us. Even the most lonely person needs to be able to spend some time alone. All of us can have too much mutuality at times. The problem is that lonely people cannot have enough, or they can get too much at one time and become overwhelmed.

If we look at loneliness, we see that it results from people-starvation. We need people who can reassure us about ourselves and help us make better assessments about the value in the world around us. We need to be able to recognize our own worth. Imagine if you don't know what your worth is. Many people who live alone feel completely worthless and insignificant. It would not make sense to take the time to get acquainted with them. If you've ever felt lonely, then you know how it feels to feel that people don't care about what you do.

There may be many reasons that we feel this, and loneliness will make them all worse. There are many reasons why people feel dissatisfied with themselves. Each reason is extremely personal. This is what makes loneliness so difficult. These personal reasons get bottled up and can quickly become out of balance. This leads to us rejecting ourselves more strongly than anyone else. It's like we are expecting to be rejected. This saves others the trouble. It's almost like we make a bet with our friends that they won't like us. If we do that, we will lose the friend we might have.

There are two possible ways to deal with loneliness. It is important to recognize the feelings of loneliness and learn how to manage them. Sometimes, it's better to learn how you can cope with the situation before trying to find a solution.

One way to deal with loneliness is by being as self-aware as possible. To get over it, you have to acknowledge the needs of your inner and outer worlds. Acceptance is the key to ending self-rejection. Sometimes we may need to learn how communicate, how give and take, in order to be able to help lonely people.

The most important thing is to remember that it is all up to us. Each of our individual contributions is important and valuable. If we can't be realistic about the value of each other, no one will be safe.

Chapter 2 The Stages of Loneliness

What causes loneliness One was asked to fill out a survey regarding loneliness among single people. The questions included those who were not married, those separated and those who were divorced/widowed. 1 completed more than a thousand questionnaires. One asked them to describe the main causes and consequences of loneliness. It was astounding to me how many answers they had. It seemed at first impossible to identify the answers. The majority of them could be divided under two main headings. They were meant to describe different situations that could lead to loneliness, and others that indicated it was a matter of personality.

CIRCUMSTANCES

People listed a few reasons why they lost contact with loved ones. Individuals who have lost contact with their loved ones due to separation from their families and friends or work from home could cite this as the cause of their loneliness. The circumstances surrounding the dissolution of a marriage (with its ending and divorce) were considered to be circumstantial. As was bereavement. Many people listed old age among the reasons. People are born to age and their friends will also become older. Even if health and strength remain intact, friends may eventually go away as they get older. Bereavement doesn't just involve the loss of a wife or husband; it can also result in the loss and deprivation of trusted friends.

Many people believed that their situations were too difficult to make friends and maintain relationships with others. They included lighthouse keepers and supervisors with remote jobs that made them feel isolated.

Many owners of small businesses work very hard but don't feel as close to their staff and never have enough time to meet up with friends. Unsocial workers include night nurses and hotel staff, who often work multiple shifts. All these people felt lonely because they were working in difficult circumstances.

A lack of friends can also result from ties or responsibilities. One woman wrote "I have an adorable dog." One is tied. Although pets can sometimes go with their owners on outings or visits to friends, it is often difficult for those who have very young children or elderly relatives to take care of. This problem is often exacerbated by the lack of financial resources.

Bus services can often be quite inefficient and expensive if you live out of town. However, many people find it financially difficult to afford the car that allows them to live in isolation. Single parents, whether they are divorced or widowed are among the hardest to hit. These single parents tend to have young children and live in small towns, villages, or hamlets. It becomes everybody's business when their sexual and social needs are met. Lack of mobility often means they are unable to get around, which can lead to them losing the social life they need to keep and make new friends.

Cultural barriers were often mentioned as barriers that are created by racial and class differences. The wrong accent can make people look different than their neighbors in certain areas. These are the areas that need to be addressed.

an indefinite sentence in prison that marks time before being released and accepted as 'one with us'. Northerners who reside in the south are mistrusted, as well as southerners who have lived in the north. A person can be identified as working class by their regional accent. This is the same today as when Shakespeare's kings and lords spoke poetry.

Soldiers using bad prose. Although the barriers seem small, they make it impossible for people to relax and feel at ease. The small rejections add to a larger number until the rejected individual gives up and gives into loneliness.

Some discriminations based on class or racial status against people are very crude. You can deal with them by just keeping your dignity and disregarding the remarks.

The most difficult are subtle discriminations.

Many of those who contributed to the survey blamed their natural tendency for loneliness. While you may be suffering from loneliness, it is important to not let others see your misery. If the mask does slip, eyebrows may be raised and you will receive a cold look. This is a clear warning to you to not let your side down and get back on track. Making a fuss will make you look good and no one will notice. These people will treat you as "a little crazy" for the rest their lives.

Many women find their social environment determined by their husbands jobs. They often move with their husbands, often leaving behind friends and neighbours they have built up a relationship with.

The husband who is promoted gets more people who respect him. The divorced wife is only able to gain the respect of strangers.

who are dependent on her every day, but need nothing from me. Both company wives and service wives can be lonely. Add to this language differences, class differences, and natural resource and you have the recipe for pain.

PERSONALITY

Many people listed various circumstances as the causes of loneliness. But, more people believed it was because of personality. Perhaps the widows and widowers are the ones who blame circumstances more. Survey respondents who had never married, and especially those men, tend to view personality as the main reason for their situation more than those who are separated or divorced.

Many people cited 'lackofconfidence' as one of their top priorities. So was afraid and afraid of strangers'. These two words can be used to refer to shyness in a variety of ways. The shy person experiences very special challenges, which will be covered in greater detail in the next chapter.

But there are still people who don't think they are shy.

Nature is not perfect. There are times when people will not trust strangers because they were hurt or let down by someone close to them. A deserted husband or wife might feel that they cannot trust anyone. One interviewee said that it was because of how they were raised. 'We kept ourselves private, and the man I trusted the most was my husband. I was alone when he abandoned me and I didn't have the experience to find strangers to help me once I got back to normal.

I was guilty of self-pity.

The notion that only some people are lonely is absurd, but it is comforting to those who feel lonely and yet are afraid of losing their friends. Loneliness can happen to anyone who is not lonely. It's much easier to just dismiss them as "that person" than it is to actually feel their discomfort.

This is why so many people identified 'handicaps' as a cause during the survey. It is apparent that physical handicaps are able to isolate people socially. People who are blind and deaf can have difficulty getting around. The added difficulty of these people is to be accepted as normal people who have normal feelings and needs.

They don't desire to be criticized, treated poorly, or ignored any more than anyone else. But it happens. When it happens to a disabled person or handicapped person, they may be able to react as if everyone else. The problem is that overreactions are too often attributed to a handicap, rather than normal feelings. After being exposed to this problem of counter-reaction and overreaction for a long period, it's easy for handicapped people to become touchy and defensive. They create a shell under which to hide and avoid company.

There are many types of handicap. Unattractive looks or poor dress are two examples of social handicaps that are often not addressed. If you don't show that you value yourself, others will not see you as valuable. People in the survey believe that lonely people are those who lack self-worth, are not attractive, do not make an effort to help others, are insignificant and uninteresting, and have some sort of personality handicap.

This myth is completely false. It is meant for those who aren't lonely and are most afraid to be alone.

EFFECTS DURING LONELINESS

I believe the survey helps us to understand loneliness as a progressive disorder that affects our personality via our communication system. I am referring to communication system. It is all the forms of 'mutual' behaviour that allow us make contact with other people and attract, sustain, and accept their attention. We also have to be able to reward them properly for the effort and time they spend. If everyone who meets you ends up believing that you are more trouble than worth their time, you will soon feel lonely. As people feel more alone, their ability to communicate with one another decreases. Communication is not about words but about emotions.

The more you cannot communicate, the less meaningful you feel. And the less useful you become to other people, because you are less able participate in mutual behaviours. Loneliness can lead to the person feeling worthless. The victim's personality has been attacked by loneliness, which attacks the communication system. He or she must stop fighting the battle and accept that the illness has won. What began as a possibility and is still a probability becomes reality.

From then on, the victim is free to drive other people away or run away from them. This protects the illness instead of destroying the person.

It is helpful and useful to think of illness as having three stages.

First is the situation that cuts people off from their friends and deprives them of mutual behavior. These are the things they do to make others feel loved, valued, or cared. They are the small, intimate things that make a difference. The victim's first stage of loneliness is when he or she feels alone and devoid of tenderness.

The first stage, or loneliness, may be enough to cause no significant damage. While it is distressing not to be able offer and accept tenderness, we can usually live with it.

It might be temporary, especially when we know how long it will take before we can have our loved ones back. We can trust that it will not last long even though we don't know. The support and comfort from other friends can help us to persevere if the person who we are waiting is very special.

Sometimes, however, the first stage can be followed by a deeper stage. The main feature of this stage is loss of confidence- self-confidence, and confidence in others. Technically, this means that the behavior becomes meaningless because the lonely person isn't able to share and receive the special forms of behaviour that can reassure us about who we are. People lose the ability to smile. People start to get less smiles and eventually stop smiling at others.

When they attempt to get things back on track, their smiles look forced and forced. It just makes matters worse. This effect isn't limited to smiling. The second stage of loneliness can affect all manner of small nonverbal behaviours. Handshakes become awkward when the victim isn't used touching people. The way you dress, your facial expressions and the speed at which you speak, how close you stand to people, how loud your voice is, the tone of the voice, the pace of speech, the speed of our speech, the rate at which we speak, the speed with the words we use, the speed at which we speak, how fast we talk, how much we smile, and the place we hang out all are affected.

The victim's confidence is slipping away in terms of his or her ability communicate with others, make and maintain contact with people so that it matters to them in a special way. Victims often blame others and it cuts them off further. Yet, others blame themselves and have the exact same effect.

Many of our thoughts oscillate between blaming the other person and blaming us.

In the third stage we are so unable to give or receive mutually beneficial behaviours that it is impossible to repair. We become apathetic, unable to feel.

It is at this stage when many of us confront the truth of our lives, and decide that no one really cares and will never care about what happens. Chronic third-stage isolation is a serious disease. Suicide may be the most extreme symptom.

It is not possible for everyone to reach the third stage. Each of us is at risk for the illness in different ways.

What is the difference between getting out of stage 1 without reaching stage 2, stage 2 without reaching stage 3, or reaching stage 3 and surviving?

One thing's certain. It's not just a matter or circumstance.

Some people lose touch with their loved ones within a matter hours and are unable to cope.

Even though they may be separated for months or years, others can still have confidence in themselves, each other and their relationship.

It must be a matter of personality. It can be caused by circumstance, but we need to understand the nature of personality to understand why some people are more susceptible. There are many other ideas than science that relate to personality.

It is common to believe that some people just are weak, that others are survivors, or that introverts are more prone to being hurt by loneliness while extroverts can simply shrug off this. These ideas are not scientific. What can we do to improve on these ideas?

The truth is that personality theories are better guesses than scientific ones. But, they're still guesses. Let's consider one way to explain personality and the reasons that some people feel more lonely than others.

A baby's brain is still in its embryonic stage. However, it has certain important abilities. Unless it is very tragic, the baby usually has well developed parts that enable them to sense touch and to see. These parts also allow the baby cry and to hear sounds. In just hours, the baby can enjoy being touched, hear noises, turn its head and respond to them. It can make faces and can quickly learn to imitate facial expressions. All of these abilities are built-in to the baby so that it can communicate basic information.

The baby is not the most important component of this equipment. It is now outdoors; the mother and father.

The adults who love the baby, take care of it, feed and look after it-in other words, the ones who will have a lot in common with the baby.

However, the majority of the baby's brain has yet to be formed. It is made up brain cells that aren't connected together.

During the first few days of life, miracles begin which help those connections grow. As it grows, baby becomes more independent as it learns about the world around him. To express its desire for attention, it may make different noises or use different faces. It will often use its entire body to talk. Not only will it be able draw attention to its needs, but it will also learn to manage that attention. Its most important behaviours are those it shares with others.

These shared experiences will enable it to learn how to communicate.

Although all babies are the same at birth they are also very different from their parents. Some mothers pay close attention to the baby's hungry cry while others ignore it until their child is ready. Mothers are different in how they feed their babies and how confident and certain they are. Fathers can be just as different. Every little thing a child experiences in life is helping to make connections in the brain. Every baby's experience is different so all connections will differ. This has its advantages. It means that the baby learns to

You will see the child behave like the parents. It will learn their language. It means that it will speak the parent's language. It does this by copying the sounds it hears and then playing around with different noises to determine what is most effective.

The baby's ability to communicate effectively within its family is evident by the time they learn to walk.

Next, it will begin to develop a vocabulary. Then, it can start to speak to its family members, siblings, and even strangers. It is important to remember that each new brain connection only works if there has been one in the past. This means that the way it behaves when it meets strangers is a continuation of the behavior it displays with its parents. Every new thing learnt applies older knowledge in new ways. As we get older, the brain's growth rate slows. But, each child is evolving into an individual, with a distinct personality. A mixture of both parents as well as any siblings or brothers with whom it communicates. The result of many influences, many unique and different circumstances.

This is how personality is formed. Communication and personality do not have to be two separate things. It's clear, however, that the first to grow is the most important component of the development of personality.

During the first few years of life. Psychologists believe that the first five-years are the most important. A person's brain has more than 50% capacity by the age 5 years. It will never be able to grow at the current rate. It might discover new ways to utilize what it has learnt, but it can't go back and erase all of its past learnings and start again with a blank slate. Brain cells, unlike all other cells in a body, never reproduce.

We can't grow new ones.

Is it possible that certain people are more susceptible to loneliness? Only time will tell. Many children may not be able to communicate in the way they are taught. Many babies are not wanted, which is a fact that many adults will need to reassure them later on in life. Parents spoil their children because they want them too. They demand more attention than they should because they were given it right at the time they needed it. Perhaps we are sometimes neglected and spoiled, but that is not the case for most of us.

Sometimes we discover we are the most valuable person in the universe, while other times we find out that we may not be.

Our personality will play a major role in how we deal with the loneliness of adulthood. How we handle the situation will depend on how well we communicated in the family situations we were born into over the years.

This is how loneliness strikes us. It won't affect us as severe if our parents choose well. The best way to demonstrate this is by looking at shyness as a problem.

Chapter 3 Feeling Shy

A shyness is often a sign of loneliness.

There are many reasons why someone might be shy. Some people are shy only when they have to, for example, at parties or dances. Everyone is looking to see how our relationship with the other sex member goes. Some of us feel shy all the while and find it extremely difficult and frightening to have a conversation. We try to think of a topic but find it impossible to express ourselves. Or they are too loud or too clumsy to be understood by others. Lonely people suffer from the lack of someone to communicate. Any form of communication with shy people can be difficult. Because a shy person may feel lonely when they are alone, it can lead to a double prison.

It helps to first accept that we all are shy at times. This means that almost everyone in the world understands how we feel, even though they don't really know how much. It's not being shy that is the problem. This understanding is usually reflected in their willingness to spend more time together than others. They will try and get you to talk. Not by laughing and trying make you forget your shyness but by listening, smiling, and giving time to try and make conversation.

There will be times when you feel the need to reject certain people, even if they seem to be trying to be kind out pity.

This is normal. Shy people dislike pity and are sensitive. The problem is that shy people mistake genuine concern for pity. They often reject kindness, believing the other person might be being hypocritical. It is easy for shy people to become trapped in trying to drive away people who understand them. It is important to first let people demonstrate that they care and want to help. People who attempt to help might be quite shy. If you reject them, it will hurt you as well.

Sometimes, it is helpful to admit that we are shy. Older people and those who seem happy and relaxed are more likely to have the time to help with shyness, as they are less in a hurry to satisfy selfish needs.

If you find someone like it, and you admit to being shy about it, you'll have someone to support you. This helps a lot at parties, social events, dances and any other type of public function. Imagine it as this: If your fear of heights is causing you to have to cross high, narrow bridges, the person who can help will be the most supportive. However, you must be open about your fears. Instead, find someone older, more sensitive, and tell the person what you are experiencing.

Then you can go to the party with that person until your confidence grows. You can begin to enjoy seeing other people having fun. This will help combat the desire to run and hide from everyone. Many people with shyness feel dizzy and confused when they do this. Loud music or a lot more movement around them can make them feel confused and dizzy. The effects fade after a while. As the brain becomes more clear, the activity around the shy person begins to make more sense. It is helpful to have someone to talk to about your shyness. Once the initial panic has subsided, it becomes easier to relax.

A lot of people are turned off by bad shyness. This prevents you and others from going out. I have known many people who are shy. Every time they try to get to social events or parties, they get lost and never find their way home. They only manage to get there just as everyone is leaving, so they have to apologize and then they go home. This is because their shyness keeps them out of the social scene and the warmth and friendliness that surrounds them. This feeling of being outsiders, not getting in until it is too much, or never showing up at all, leaves the shy person feeling stupid and unimportant.

But being shy can also keep you from being perceived as foolish or clumsy. Also, it can make you a social failure. This is probably the whole reason shyness exists. It is a form protection. It stops shy people from making errors. Many shy people feel that they're foolish, unattractive, and clumsy.

They have a low opinion of their worth and attempt to convince others not to care about them. If you feel this way about you, you will be tempted not to let people reject you and to reject yourself before you have the chance to meet them.

Let us say that you are like the following. What can be done? The best thing you can do is admit your shyness. However, this will likely make it more difficult.

If you're like this, it is likely that you were taught to shyness by your parents or other family members. This is not as simple as it seems. Each person learns as a child what to expect and how to draw attention to make them feel safe and secure. Some children are safer when they don't draw any attention. They learn to ignore the adults around them and to avoid being noticed. It only leads to violence, sarcasm, and disputes between their parents. The parents will have their own problems.

To this type of parent, having a child around can be an annoying nuisance and embarrassment. The child is taught to put up a good example and to remain quiet. The child learns it is safer to pretend that it does not exist. Its parents have taught him to be shy and not risk offending anyone.

These children often experience a very lonely childhood. But even less severe cases can cause very bad shyness. Sometimes parents allow the child to be noticed, but in limited ways.

This is what happens when the spoilt little one has everything, but is never expected be content. Soon, the spoilt child learns to please his parents by demanding more and more. It only needs to say, "I Want", and it gets another present. However, presents from such parents cannot replace love. This is when parents do not love one other and cannot be open about their feelings. They give the child materialistic things, instead of the warmth and friendship they need. The parents of the spoilt kid are often sexually anxious of one another and fear strong feelings. Each temper tantrum is a frightening experience for them. They give in to the child's demands because they are able to avoid showing any emotion to each other.

The child is aware that it is not receiving true love, and that each present will be followed with another.

So the child knows that the gifts are not valuable and it works out that love is hollow. This is how the child learns that love can be a very ineffective commodity and is therefore a useless person. Tantrums often result in bribes and presents during childhood. The tantrums end up working against other people in adolescence. The spoilt child becomes irritable and expects that this will attract attention. Although this is a temporary strategy that works, sooner or later the child will start to collect rejections. He or she becomes shy and sulky and avoids people.

Although they may be happy and healthy parents, there are some who are not too fussy with their children. This can lead you to a different kind of shyness than 'don't exist'shyness or'sulky'shyness. These parents will be the ones whose whole attitude can be summed up by the words "Don't touch". They will never or very rarely cuddle their children. Cuddling, putting their arms around their children and holding on tight to them, is often confused with coddling. The child becomes weak and cowardly. Some families still teach boys to not show pain, discomfort, or to cry. These actions are considered unmanly. They can also lead to homosexuality. A few girls are also taught that emotions should not be displayed as weakness or foolishness. Their parents are concerned that their daughters will grow up as little dolls filled with feminine nonsense and make their bodies easy prey for greedy sexual adventurers. Sometimes the parents really wanted to have a boy and were not happy with the choice of having a child. The parents raised their daughter to look more like a boy.

These children, although not always shy, are sometimes raised in this manner. Some children may be more shy-sexually assertive and shallow than others. Others become shy when they see others affectionately.

They do not know what it means when a charming person of their own age wants them to hug and kiss them. They can't stop freezing up and want to run away. When parents say "Don't touch", it means "don't sexually touch". Even the slightest flirtation or advances can make a child blush and feel guilty. They don't understand the value of physical and emotional love. Instead, their parents are too proud to show their affection by cuddling up with them. They fear that their normal sexual fantasies will lead them to betray their deepest desires and drive away the people who they like. They refuse to accept rejection for being too openly sexual.

They are warm and seductive inside and want to be held and reassured. However, the outside is cold and untouchable.

How can someone like this help themselves? The people who were taught not that they exist need to find someone who will give them permission and who will be open to making mistakes and anger. People who are sulky, or shy and were raised poorly, need to be able to believe that they are worth the chance of finding true and lasting relationships. It's important to relearn how to touch, and to be touched, the "cold outsiders" who yearn to be warm inside. But how does each one do this?

The formula for success doesn't take long to learn.

Acceptance of how they came to be shy is the first step. You may find this possible when you have a deeper understanding about your parents' problems. An angry adult with his or herself can make it difficult to see that the parents were not trying to harm their child. They may have done so by accident, while struggling with their own deep unhappiness. A lot of shyness stems from anger and resentment because our parents are too busy with other things to care for us. This is simply not the right way to see things. They did not choose problems. Nobody likes having problems. They would rather not have been in these situations.

Even if you suffer, it is because they tried. In the end, you had to go through heartbreak and conflicts you could not understand. Now you're old enough for understanding, empathy and forgiveness.

Second, treating shyness of this nature takes time.

It does not matter if your shyness is due to being taught not to exist, never to expect genuine affection, or not to show feelings. No shining knight or beautiful princess will rescue you. You must learn from your mistakes and go it alone. Learning from your mistakes is the only way you can improve. You'll learn from them, not your parents', this time.

Third, let's not forget what shyness does. It protects you from potential risks, but it also causes us to become very angry and afraid of expressing our anger. Turning our anger inwards is the best way to deal with it. Allow some anger to flow. The effect will be surprising. The effect will be recognized by everyone else you want to meet because they all had the same problem growing up. They will appreciate your feelings and allow you to share them. Don't be afraid to speak up and let others know how you feel.

Fourth, take time to look at yourself. Shy people are almost always attractive, and many are very beautiful.

There is a good reason. Shyness is rooted early in life and hinders an early rise into adulthood. A lot of shy people look charming and childlike. Their eyes are big, their skin is soft, and they have a charm smile that makes them seem modest and sincere. These qualities are very appealing in an individual's look. Not all beauty is necessary. In fact, even if you have very odd features, your eyes and mouth can still be quite attractive. The shy who can't live with others and the sulky shy don't smile very often and are often afraid to pout. Their faces can often be quite striking and attractive. If you smile a lot, you can run the risk that your words will be misunderstood. It's nothing to be afraid of, you'll discover.

Smile back at them and you're well on your way. The don'ttouch shy tend to be good at smiling, and bad at eye.

contact. If you feel shy, try looking at the other person more. But, don't forget to let the corners crinkle. Practice with a mirror. This isn't hypocritical, immoral, contrived, or harmful. Let's have a look, but please don't frown.

The worst problem with shyness, however, is that many shy people actually enjoy being shy. In fact, shyness can take many forms. It is more rewarding for the shy person to fail to conquer their shyness rather than to try to defeat it. When this happens, shyness can become a serious illness.

Consider, for example, the compulsive player. He or she gambles all day and always loses. Although the gambler claims he or she is doing it to make money, the psychological reward of losing money keeps the illness going. In the same way, an alcoholic claims that he doesn't enjoy the consequences of drinking, but rather the pleasure of the initial stages of drinking.

The problem with alcoholism is not the desire to feel dirty or degraded afterwards. Many people who are shy are just like them. Failure is a reward for them. They are allowed to fail socially by their shyness; not because they make a mess of it, but because that is an acceptable reason for being shy.

Short-term failures due to shyness are often rewarded when our closest and dearest make a big fuss of us, and say that at the very least we tried, we're improving, and don't fret, maybe it was for good.

All the talking and consolation can be very enjoyable-much better than risking that someone else will not like us. Parents who have shy children are more likely to reward the illness than the child. They do it because they are alone and shy, and don't want their child growing up and loving someone else. This is something they sometimes admit to, but it is usually not true. What can you expect from your parents? Recognizing that you are entitled to your rights and no one can take them away is the best thing. This might hurt your parents initially. They will get used to it. They will eventually understand that it is better to hurt them less than you do in the long term. You can explain your rights to them gently, assure them, then move to a faraway fiat or home. You can learn to live by yourself. However, you need to keep an eye on the other person to make sure they're not feeling lonely. Your loneliness is not their problem. Even if we do not help others immediately, in the end, we must solve our own problems.

We have so far focused on the worst types shyness. These are the ones which we learn about as children due to the close relationship that our parents have. We can overcome the milder forms of shyness, although they are still very painful.

The first is shyness towards certain situations.

Some people are shy when they go out to eat or stay at a hotel. This could be because they are afraid of doing something wrong. Perhaps their parents were not good at taking them out. This is a simple question. It's easy to do. Everyone feels awkward the first times they try something new. Next time will come easier, and then the next one even more.

A second factor is shyness towards certain types people: the attractive and beautiful, as well as those who are wealthy, powerful, or famous. Remember that these people are just people, and they may be just as nervous.

People often only see beauty in a beautiful person, and not the real person who lives inside. The chance to get acquainted with an ordinary person is something few people have. A person who makes you feel nervous at first can often be very grateful to be treated just like any other person. It is easier to communicate normally when you are interested in listening, talking, and showing interest in others. The rich and powerful also like to be considered ordinary human beings.

This is their reality. They can help you feel more at peace, especially if they have been used to meeting people with shiny, bright eyes. However, you may be worried that your expectations may be too high. Part of your desire to have more control is if you are extremely attracted. Fear not!

They are already used to this, so it is not surprising that they can lose some control.

A third factor is that certain events can make it worse.

People may feel embarrassed by the pub, dance and disco. Perhaps the talk is too superficial or too loud.

Not better, alcohol can make matters worse. In fact, alcohol can make things worse than they are! You might feel like running or standing still. These situations are best avoided if they don't work for you. The same applies to parties. Do not engage in small talk if this is something you do not enjoy. Be serious and avoid being boring.

Your talk will become more interesting as you continue to work on it.

The majority of people who are shy in this world are probably the majority. They manage to overcome it, no matter how young they are. Sometimes sexual ignorance and fear can make shyness worse. While everyone in the so-called permissive society should know about sex and how it works, love of sex can only be learned through real life experiences. Shy people don't often fear sex. They are sensitive people who, rightly, are afraid of being given meaningless sex rather than loving sex. The little things, such as holding hands and talking to one another, are crucial. Is it a sign that he loves me, or just that he wants to have sex with me? The dilemma of how far you will go is the hardest part for sexually shy people. There is no quick solution.

You must take your time, be patient and get used the feeling of holding hands before moving on. If the other person can't understand you and doesn't respect you for it then he/she is not the right person. As an aside, shy women often believe they are being misunderstood because they are sexually stimulated slowly. They are often tempted to believe that too. The truth is that most women have a slow rate of sexual satisfaction until they feel comfortable with someone. Shy women are not at all unusual. They just need confidence, as with all of us, before they are able to commit to something.

Chapter 4 Communication improvement

Loneliness, a form of loneliness, is a disorder that hinders people's ability communicate and take part on mutual behaviors.

Because of the way they were raised, shy people can be particularly vulnerable. Communication is a key factor in how vulnerable each of us are to loneliness. Although communication may be something we learned in childhood or later, we all can improve our ability to communicate. We've looked at communication in general. Now, it's time to get into the details. This chapter could be called 'How you can improve your resistance towards loneliness'.

We already know that communication's purpose is to make people feel better. We also noticed that there are four types of behaviours that are particularly involved in communication: talking and listening, looking at, touching and looking. When we look at communication, we need to take a closer look at how they help us understand what another person thinks and feels.

It is impossible to know for sure what someone else thinks or feels. We can make guesses and, if our knowledge of the other person is good, have high chances of being accurate, we can sometimes be quite certain that our guesses are correct. This is achieved by being aware of non-verbal communication behaviours of other people, and listening to words and verbal behaviours. So, we don't just pay attention to what someone is saying, but also the context, meaning that it makes sense. Verbal behaviour-how people say things-makes much more sense if you take into consideration who is saying them, when they are being said and in what circumstances. Even though we cannot see the meaning of people not using words, we can still see that they may be saying something very important. Silences are powerful.

There are six main types of nonverbal behaviour.

First, there are many body movements. These help us to judge how someone is feeling and to predict what their next actions will be. There are also non-verbal characteristics that relate to the way someone uses their eyes. Mutual eye contact is the most important. It involves both parties looking at each other directly. Thirdly, touch is an intimate and powerful form that allows people to communicate with each other.

The fourth category includes communication speech patterns. These include changes in tone and volume, loudness of speech, lengths of pauses, and other such things.

Fifth: How space is used for communication.

Not Outer Space. It is the inner space between two people. We respond differently to public and personal space.

Finally, man-made things are used by everyone to define their 'image'. We use our clothes and hairstyles as well as our cars and homes. Of course, artifacts are used to express status or to show the lack thereof,'stigma.

It is important that you understand each of these behaviors because loneliness can cause changes in the way people communicate with one another.

While there isn't yet any direct evidence to support this statement in fact, there is plenty of evidence that friends produce different behaviours from strangers. Another obvious characteristic of lonely people, however, is the lack of friends to communicate with. It is useful to discuss how illness like loneliness can cause non-verbal communication to be distorted.

BODY MOVEMENTS

Communication can be achieved by a variety of body movements.

Gait, stance, seance. How we walk and stand can often tell others how we feel. In the early days of experimental psychology, around ten years back, this subject was being studied. Scientists hoped that they could create a dictionary of what was then known as body language. According to scientists, it could be possible to say that, for example if someone sits with his legs crossed and arms folded, with his head at a certain angle, this could be related in a sentence, such 'I despise all of you' or 'I hope you will change the topic'. They abandoned their search slowly. There doesn't appear to be a common language between the bodies, except in very general terms. Or in terms of abstract, not very useful biological signs that owe more science to zoology to understanding the feelings of people.

It is easier to use these non-verbal signals and body movements for guesswork. After we have guessed what someone is thinking or feeling, we watch to see if they can give us more clues. Sometimes we try to infer another person's behaviour, and other times we do the same thing.

Imagine walking into a room crowded with strangers. It is important to not attract attention to yourself by your way of walking. You will appear tentative. You will look nervous and be cautious about bumping into furniture or other objects. You will likely avoid walking in public spaces where everyone will be able watch every step you take. There's a good chance that your eyes will not be drawn to people. On the other side, if you wish for everyone to notice your presence, you will not just come into the room. You will move slowly and deliberately into the public space. Then you will gather everyone's attention until they stop talking.

Your manner of walking, standing, and sitting will tell others how confident you are. If you want to make people feel more confident than they actually are, you have to act confidently and appear completely at ease.

This can be extremely difficult for some people, especially if they are speaking to an audience or during an interview. Relaxation is key. Deep breathing lowers the body's natural defences. It produces less chemicals that can make it easy to run away from home or be aggressive. It is possible to relax more if you take some deep breaths before you start taking your next few deep breaths. Another part of this answer is to recognize that the nervousness that you feel is more noticeable to yourself than it is for the audience. They will almost always make allowances for what you are feeling and will be there to support your cause.

Many of them understand that they would be nervous if placed in your shoes. They will also sympathize with what you are going through.

For lonely people, walking, standing, and sitting can be used to demonstrate their loneliness. They are not interested in sharing their behaviours. They can be too passive or active, and they can also be aggressive.

Second stage loneliness appears to be often displayed deliberately so that sufferers seem like they are saying, "Look at myself, I am lonely." So please don't disturb me.

It is almost like they have a small cage that they keep with them. They don't allow us to get our fingers stuck in the bars, unless we want to either be bitten by them or pointly ignored. A first stage lone lie can often lead to an exaggerated desire for people to talk. They walk too fast and interfere with other people's lives, withdrawing unpredictably. They sit so often that they seem to be constantly listening to other people's conversations. Third stage victims are able to walk and stand alone in their own world and not be aware of the existence of others.

Facial expression. Every person learns to imitate others' facial expressions in their early years. We also begin to make our own. When most of us reach adulthood, we can use the muscles on our face in many ways. However, we often limit ourselves to just a few expressions. This habit leads to our faces becoming creased, marked and difficult to predict by those who are familiar with us.

A person's ability and ability to respond to subtle facial signals is affected by loneliness. Understanding the origins of these signals can help to reduce this effect. You can see the three main areas in facial muscle if you look at yourself in a mirror. When these muscles are relaxed and tightened, our faces change. Big changes generate loud, or extremely large signals. But small changes create soft, or subtle signals.

The corrugators are the topmost muscle group.

They are located below the skin on the forehead. If you lift these up, the skin becomes swollen or corrugated.

This is done by lifting your eyebrows as high and far as possible. Another set of tiny muscles creates a vertical fold above the spot where the nose and forehead meet. There are many factors that affect the appearance of your face. Some people have more of a vertical crease than others.

There are several groups of muscles around the eyes. To discover how they function, all you have to do is close your eyes and open them slowly.

You can keep opening them until you reach the point where they open naturally. Relax. Do this exercise three to four more times and you won't feel the strain.

The corners of our mouth are the final set of facial muscles. You can strengthen them again by performing an exercise. The first thing you can do is pull your muscles back by exaggerating the use of the word'me. You should feel your corners getting closer together.

Next, pronounce "you" by pushing your lips out front as far and as high as you can.

People who are shy tends to overuse their facial muscles. This happens less to people who are lonely. Flabby muscles tend to be less active. It is as important as to strengthen facial muscles so that they can work for a living. Once they feel strong and ready to go, you can use them as necessary. One great exercise is the slow smiling. Begin by placing your lips down as far as you can. Next, move slowly (over a minute if it's possible) to lift the corners upwards and create a full smile.

All of these exercises don't help us make the right signs when we meet someone.

It is to enable us all to produce signals. Loneliness makes it difficult for people to respond to messages.

The smile is a common early death as the illness advances.

Smiling, a fun activity, should bring joy to your face.

It works best when it's spontaneous and full of unconscious confidence. It is better to smile contrived than not smile at all. It is possible to tone those smile-muscles that have lost their strength due to inactivity.

Gesture. Gesture. This includes the use your hands to demonstrate what you are saying. It's important to remember that artificial gestures can be awkward and embarrassing.

Relaxed gestures are more natural and easier.

An individual who is highly self-conscious tends to gesticulate in an awkward, contrived manner or appear stiff and clumsy. Use of gesture should be simple, clean, elegant, and decisive. The best preparation for a successful career is to maintain a healthy body and engage in movement exercises and music at school.

Yoga is an excellent way to help you do this. To feel at home within our bodies, we don't need to fear. It's easy to let it all happen. Trusting your body and being happy in it is the best foundation for confidence.

Synchrony Movements. Small body movements help people stay comfortable when they talk with each other. They may move slightly, such as swaying back and forth or shifting their position when they are seated. Each movement is often timed in a way that fits together, which makes slow motion look like synchrony movements. Because they are coordinated, each movement can be called synchrony. These movements help us tell if someone's paying attention to what we say or do. If the movements are no longer synchronized, they can be taken to indicate that they are no longer interested.

When you are in the initial stage of loneliness, there is temptation to want to change the behavior of the other person. We should instead take our time, get to know theirs, then try to adapt our patterns to them. People need time to become comfortable with each other, particularly if they are distant or unfamiliar. An analysis of strangers meeting first shows that it takes between four and five minutes before the behaviour, particularly the synchronized movement, settles down into an acceptable pattern, in which both become more comfortable with one another. The more lonely we are, it is important to take the time to get to grips with others and, more importantly, let them get to know you. Instead of spending four or five mins, we'll need eight or ten. It is more than just listening to the words. You must also let your interest show through the movement. To allow our natural rhythm of synchrony to return to its natural rhythm, it is important to try to forget our own problems.

MUTUAL EYE CONTACT

When two people look at each other, they make contact in a way that is similar to touching.

Contact between strangers might be very brief. This contact is more lasting when people know each others well enough to be friends or lovers. There is a difference between looking into each others eyes and looking into theirs. When two people make eye contact, it means they have combined their individual attention systems into one. As if one were to inspect the eyes of another person for flaws, it will produce a very different result. Although they have not created a new system of mutual attention, they still work individually. Mutuality will be destroyed if one of them is more active than the others.

This is why lonely people don't have the experience to create a common system. They find it difficult to connect and maintain the connections that they have made. This may be because they often make eye contact but are not using it to excuse smiling or having a chat. Part of this problem is

The most important thing (to be dealt about later) is knowing the right words to use. The biggest problem is knowing how to say it. You can take a signal as being too aggressive or strong or as weak and uninterested if it's not. Only practice will make it right.

You can do this by giving back a little less than you receive. But not excessively! You would rush the other person. It's like taking the hand instead if shaking it.

It allows people to communicate with each other by keeping their eyes open at the most comfortable distance. It can also help people know what to expect. In any conversation speech is shared. Eyes are used to indicate when the other person should speak. If we look away from the speaker after they have finished speaking and do not look back at them, this could mean we aren't interested in what the person has to share. If we focus on the person speaking, and then look up at them closely, we will be showing an increase in interest. Our partner will interpret this as a sign of a significant moment. It will appear that we have something important to say, and the other person should follow suit. This can often be taken as a sign that we have nothing to add and are not interested in continuing the conversation.

TOUCHING

The handshake is probably the most common form to person-to-person touch between strangers. It is normal to say, "I'm delighted to meet with you!" When shaking hands, it is standard to say "I'm delighted to meet your!" If you want the handshake to mean anything, it is vital that we truly are pleased and this is displayed. It is more effective if you show the same amount of pleasure as the person with whom you are hand-holding.

How do people touch to express their feelings?

There are three major factors that influence how we touch: its duration, intensity, frequency, and frequency. As an example, when we touch our hands, it can be a long or short handshake. The more time it takes to turn into handholding, the more it will last.

A continental handshake can be very formal and brief. American handshakes last longer than British ones. The intensity can vary widely.

Some people can produce strong handshakes. While others may produce weaker ones of the wet fish variety, some people do it very strongly. It doesn't matter how many times we shake hands.

Imagine meeting someone and shaking hands eighteen to nine times.

In general, there are three kinds touch: the type that makes an immediate impact; the type which increases pressure; or the one we caress. Some touch types, such as cuddling or cuddling, can use all three. Others, such the nudge and cuddling, use only touch.

Another important aspect to touching is how we touch. Strangers love to be touched on the cheek rather than with a handshake. The truth is that everyone has places they are very protective of. This fascinating aspect in human sexuality is one we cannot really explore. We will just say that all touch must give pleasure and be pleasant to do. However, without mutual pleasure it will often be rejected. This can be very dangerous for lonely patients, especially those who are in the third or second stages of their illness. It is very easy to avoid touch, be too greedy or take too much for granted.

Loneliness is a deprivation of the experience of touching and being touched. It's difficult to reduce this deprivation by social convention without being misunderstood. Adults also need to know they are loved and can be touched, just like babies.

PATTERNS REGARDING SPEECH

One simple sentence can be taken as an example and used millions of thousands of times each day. There are many possible ways that it could be said. First, the speed at the which the words can be pronounced can vary. This allows us to speak quickly or slowly. The volume of the words can be changed to make it more or less loud. We can pause at any point between words. Also, the length of these stops can be changed. One or more of the following words can be highlighted: 'I'm pleased you meet you', or I'm glad you meet me!' There are many accents that can be used to express the words. There are many ways to change the tone of your voice. This allows you to speak in a pleasant, angry, timid or confident manner.

Do you know of thousands of ways to make money? There must be billions. And each of us can choose from many of these.

So how do you decide how to communicate something? Evidently, some of that decision is taken for us, and not by we.

Most of us learn one language at a time, with one accent. The accent is often a clue about where we are from. It can also tell you the region we live in and the class to whom we belong.

We have two options: we can either minimize it or exaggerate. Your situation and the person that you are speaking with will probably determine your choice. Most people do not have a lot of options, and they would prefer to not be hidden.

People use your speed, intonation and volume to assess the type of person you are dealing with. Most people know someone who talks in a loud voice and someone who talks softly.

There are fast and slow speakers. There are two types of people: rapid talkers and slow talkers.

It is generally assumed that their speaking style speaks volumes to their personality. People who speak slow are often viewed as slow-witted. On the other side, those with fast speaking skills are viewed as being too clever or a confidence tricker.

It is very likely that loneliness can affect how people talk because they have lost the ability to interact with others. It can be difficult for people who aren't used talking to figure out how fast they talk, how loud they talk and when it's time to stop. You can also notice a change in your voice. Because depression affects our ability to communicate with others. Many lonely people find that they are more sensitive about the speed and volume at which others speak. Shy people tend to be more sensitive than others. It can be hard to assess what people say about us and ourselves when we talk to them, especially if they aren't used talking to us. Tension builds up and we retreat in our own selves, afraid to make a wrong decision that might draw attention to ourselves. You may feel that nobody is talking with you and everyone else is talking about your self-confidence. Let us take our time and remember that we are not inherently flawed. The key is to focus on listening until you are ready to talk.

SPACE and PROXIMITY

There is a natural distance that allows for comfortable conversation. While it can vary from country country to country, three to four feet is usually sufficient. Queues tend towards being more spread out to ensure that the people in them are not too close.

Every so often, someone will try and get too close for their comfort. In these instances, we must decide whether to remain firm or stand our ground. People are more comfortable talking in groups of twos when they sit down, especially for informal conversations. In this situation, their angle is more important than their distance. People who are not close to one another tend to not choose face-toface positions. Instead they will have ninety degrees of separation between their lines. This allows them to each turn away naturally, and without seeming to do so intentionally. To turn away deliberately looks like rejection.

Unfortunately, many environments in public places can hinder comfortable conversation. This is often made worse with high levels, distracting noises, and excessive crowding.

People who would like to speak in private in public spaces prefer background noise. It allows them to be certain that nothing they say is being listened to. However, many people feel that pubs should be seen as places where they can make friends. Many of them encourage loneliness.

ARTIFACTS USE

All non-verbal behaviour can serve as the basis of guesswork about someone's meaning. These include the clothes we wear, our hairstyles, and the way we present us.

Neglected people may appear as though their needs are being ignored, or as if they would prefer to be treated as if they were. It is possible for spoiled people to appear as though they are expecting more. However, appearances often reflect a person's true nature. People can be deceived by their appearances.

What can non-verbal behaviour do to improve our ability to communicate with others. On the surface, it seems to have the opposite effect. When we focus too much on our own behavior we may retreat further from other people. However, this can happen. It is not something that lasts. One of the consequences of loneliness is that it reduces our ability for communication and helps us to deal with others. Just as with any other skill we get rusty if we try to begin again. All skills are complex, consisting of many small behaviours which the confident performer takes unconsciously for granted. It takes practice before confidence can be restored. This means practice with all the skills and careful attention to each sub-skill. However, failure is not an option. It's only by making mistakes and learning from them that we can correct them. Learning can come from failure.

Chapter 5 Young and lonely

The first stages in loneliness are almost always linked with certain circumstances. If it is adults, their susceptibility will depend on how well they can cope with it. The experience of being alone in childhood is a factor that many believe is crucial. It is possible to argue that all children experience being alone as they age and that it is good for them to learn how to manage their own affairs. This could be true. But it seems cruel, unwise, and impractical to inflict harm on another person, particularly a child, purely for the sake or doing good. There is a significant difference between feeling lonely in a single moment and being isolated all the time. Many lonely adults can attribute their inability or inability of coping with loneliness to long periods spent alone as children. Their parents didn't care enough to notice the distress and did not pay attention to it.

Graeme's story highlights the difficulties that lonely children face. He was born 1952 to his mother in her mid-twenties. His father, who was thirty years old, was an Assistant Manager in a shoe store. His parents were ambitious and determined that he would travel the world to obtain better material circumstances. Graeme may have moved from one place to another as a child, never settling at one school or one of his friends. When his father was promoted, they would move to larger houses in strange places. His mother worked at many different jobs, so her son was expected to return home from school to get into a strange place and make his own meals. He wrote, "I learned how to cook for myself," but he was sure he still resents it. His parents were often at odds and it was not uncommon for the house to be chaotic. "They would stop speaking to eachother, not have rows, shout at each others, and just ignore what each said." I did not know how to please them so in the end, I decided to go my own way. I've always been a bit lonely as a consequence.

There was no doubt that Graeme had loved his parents. They were each different, but they ultimately ignored him. Graeme experienced a nervous breakdown as a teenager. He had fought against inadequacies in his schooling to be able to attend university. But he couldn't keep up. "I needed the social lives. My problem was that my understanding of friendship and how to keep them was lacking. My work was compromised, and then I fell deeply in love with a girl that had many admirers and little time for myself. Later, I found out that she looked very similar to my mother as a young woman. My mother was also busy with many other things and little time for us. The greatest joke was that I once tried telling my father how I had grown up, and he replied that he had taken care of everything so I could have an even better childhood than the one he had. He expected me even to be grateful.

Ellen, now in their forties, recalls a difficult childhood. She was surrounded by older brothers and a younger sister. She explained that her father believed strongly in Victorian virtues. Children should never speak to each other until they are spoken to. They should also be seen and not heard. Her mother treated her very coldly and it was only much later that she was finally able to find an explanation. Ellen was born a year before her parents parted ways. "My mother disliked me. This could have been because her father was not there or because she returned in disgrace to be with me. Before her death, she did tell me that she had always disliked me and that we became friends for a while. It was helpful to learn why, but I will never be able to make up for that childhood.

Even now, though I am able to trust others, I still don't really know how.

They will probably reject me, I'm sure. Perhaps I choose people that I don't like. Ellen was a scapegoated kid, who assumed all the responsibility for the family's problems.

Despite having two disastrous marriages, she now has her own daughter.

What can one do to help these children who are alone? Unfortunately, the people who are most vulnerable are those whose families are directly to blame, but are not able to see the real damage they are doing. Sometimes they are ambitious as Graeme's parents. Sometimes it is just that the two of you don't get along. Friends, teachers, neighbours, or neighbors cannot interfere without doing more injury than good. Teachers and friends can be there to offer support and friendship to the child.

Ellen found consolation and comfort in a friendship that she shared with an elderly man who lived just down the road. She said that her uncle used to make models to sell toys. He said, "We just got along. He let him do the fetching and carrying, holding bits of wood as he glued them. I went on about how awful I hated my mom, and he listened.

Then he died. I was just ten. That was it. My last friend. But I'll never forget him.'

Teachers can do a lot during school, but the first step in helping lonely children is to find them. He or she isn't likely to draw attention. Lonely, or at least partially isolated children, are more often in the middle than at the bottom of the ability scale. They hide their feelings of social isolation by staying close to people rather than moving away. It is a tendency to exaggerate about their own lives that is most shocking. A nursery class girl who is up-and-coming politician's daughter, played it out by pretending she owned a pet rabbit. She was very lonely and her parents were always dismissive. Later, she confessed to her teacher that there were many of her siblings and could not see them all.

The lonely children that make up imaginary companions don't always feel lonely. However, the teacher can look into this and help the child find the right extra something in the classroom to help him trust others.

It is common for young people to not like or trust other people. This can lead to loneliness. This is when we are expected or required to get married. If you're a young lady, your parents can be some of the most loving people you know. But, they can also make it difficult to see the inward side of you by how they try so hard to avoid the subject of marriage while still making it very clear that this is what they want. Men hear wedding bells as soon as you mention a male. This impression suggests that it doesn't matter who you get married to, so long it is males and of your age. "What happened with that nice boy I brought home last year?" This is quickly followed by

'Perhaps, you don't play your cards correctly! As if husbands weren't people you might spend your whole life with, but rather some kind of prize that can be won in a bizarre form of strip-poker.

You may not realize it, but your parents often comment on the choice of their partner. However, the truth is that your marriage should be your own. It can be done with your ideas and expectations.

Young men are just the same victims of their parents' ideas on marriage as young ladies. Today, more men are married than women in their younger years. So, it's not the women who are most likely end up on the shelf, but the men.

You will always be reminded, regardless of your sexual orientation, that you are single if below thirty-five and are not married. Advertising is almost exclusively geared towards couples, and even couples with kids. Singles pay higher taxes. People assume you must be in some sort of trouble if your spouse is not yet married. Parties are a lost and confused search for someone who can be interesting in spite of all the noise. If you're not yet settled enough or aren't motivated enough to take on more responsibility, even promotion can be held back. It is quite insulting to look for a single pork cut in the supermarket, only to discover that they are all available in pairs- the big one for him or the little one.

Although it is funny, loneliness can often be difficult for young people who are not married. It can lead to loneliness that becomes too chronic and consuming. How you live is important. It's worse to be alone. It's far better to be around people and have conversations with them at night. There should be something for us to come home to. We need to have an interest or hobby that we can continue at home.

So that you can hear your favorite song when you return to home, leave the best track on the hifi. The end of the jigsaw or the last chapter of an exciting book should be kept. Also make sure to have someone to talk with at work, or over the phone at night.

While you will always feel the 'nasties,' that feeling that your life has been a total waste of effort and that it would not matter if you died, there are times when you just need to be reminded that this is normal. A friend to talk to is more than a means of coping with these feelings. Being a chatty friend is worth more than being sad to. It's important to have someone you can communicate with in a casual and light-hearted manner.

Media portrays being single in big city as the ideal recipe for carefree pleasure. They see the happy bachelor and the hopeful spunster running from party to bar with their high disposable incomes. They have a lot of fun, don't worry about anything, and can take full advantage our permissive society. Personally, I don't believe it is. I believe that singles, especially those unmarried in their 20s and 30s, are more lonely than most of the city's older people who can look back on accomplishments and other adventures.

We have already discussed a lot of what to do when we first meet someone we take seriously. How can we meet them first? One way to make it happen is through commercially operated organizations. However, there are events that take place in large cities. They help people meet people, whether they want to expand their network of friends or find potential spouses. What are the pros and cons of each contact method? Is it best for people who are struggling with loneliness or who want to stay hopeful?

COMPUTER DATING

Nearly everybody who is lonely will admit they are searching for that special someone, the one person who will always be right for them. Computer dating appeals to people who feel they know exactly what kind of person will be their perfect match and believe they can find that person quicker and more efficiently by using computers than letting the universe take their course.

It's not hard to find the computer dating site. There are many advertisements. But, can a computer company help you find your soulmate?

It is best to get to know how the system works before you start spending money on online dating. Your address is as valuable to the firm as any other mail order business. You are likely to continue receiving communications from them for some time, regardless of whether you sign up or not. It's a high-priced service, so it's worth knowing what you'll be paying if joining.

Computer dating services operate in roughly the same way. First, the client fills out a questionnaire. He or she gives details about themselves and the person they are looking for. The client must provide information about his/her physical characteristics, as well as the sociological categories (such things like age, height and weight, skin colour and religion). They then list the individual's interests and preferred activities. Some of them include what appears to be psychological tests which show the personality traits of the person.

Most often, such "tests" are just cosmetic. Both for technical reasons that will be clear soon and because the companies seldom employ psychologists as a way to interpret such tests.

The disadvantages are much more difficult to evaluate than the merits.

First, there are better chances of you receiving names if your area has many members.

Living in a big city puts you at a disadvantage. A second factor is the fact that women between 20 and 30 years old are more likely to have two men than their female counterparts. Being male puts you at an disadvantage. Thirdly, because this questionnaire and advertising emphasize that it is a way to find a partner of your dreams, there is an inherent tendency for people not only to visualize the person they are looking for in their answers, but also to make a positive image of themselves. However, the truth may be very different. It is possible to meet people who might not look like you imagined. People lie about their years. People also alter their height, weight, habits, and behavior to achieve the perfect image they desire.

Computer dating agencies know they must create the impression that they have a large and diverse membership. It is best to be skeptical of any claims made by these companies. In deciding whether or no computer finds someone for you, where you live is most important. Age is the second most important. You won't mind the age of anyone you meet. It will make it easier to find people for you.

This is, despite being a blind-date scenario. It will still be blinding in one way, as your ideal self was matched up with another person's. This may result in very different realities when the two meet.

Nonetheless, the system does have its successes. Or maybe it has more successes than that. The real benefit lies with those who can spare the money, who are interested not only in making contacts with their predestined love, but also in making friends and making friends with strangers.

Ironically, they are the least likely to need the service and have the easiest of cases.

There is no doubt that being young and lonely in any country or big city is a very different kind of hell. It helps to be around other people. But ultimately, it is up to each individual to determine what they want and then to develop the skills to accomplish that.

Chapter 6 The Middle Years and Loneliness

In our society that is permissive, for most people, the ideals associated with marriage rule the twenties, if not the thirties. The desire to marry becomes a defining characteristic for those who have not yet married. Those who aren't interested in getting married see themselves as "on the list", while those who do get married are constantly reminded of how odd they look to others. We are all likely to have some experience with marriage by the time we reach age 35.

The reality is that many people's marriages have not turned out the way they expected. Some are happy to stay married and endure their troubles. Some of them are secretly involved in affairs. Others are married and could divorce. There are also increasing chances of getting married after the age 30.

The threat of loneliness can pose a threat to each of these populations. Despite current myths, it is just about as likely that the disease will strike married victims. It's worse to live with someone you don't know than to be married. One wife wrote the following:

Although most people see us as happy, stable, and happy couples, the pain of loneliness is part of daily life. My husband is a good guy, but the wrong one. I can't get him to understand the frustration and incompatibility that drives me mad.

He has everything, and I have only a few days left. My children may be able to give me pleasure and go their way, but I am unable to share with them all the things that are so enjoyable. Without retreating into my own solitary prison, I feel trapped. I find it most frustrating to go to bed at night, as that is when my feelings of being trapped are greatest.

Many times, the lonely wife, who appears to be happy married and not divorced from her husband, gets treated as depressed by her doctor and given tranquillizers. The causes cannot be addressed. And while it is true, no doctor can diagnose them for someone like that, more doctors might offer encouragement through good counselling so the person can start to tackle the problems. What are the causes

There are two types of causes. The first group of causes is in the marriage itself. Many reasons people get married, but the primary reason is to make a commitment to each other and become better people.

As long as one partner isn't too rapid for the other, it can work. Many men and women feel threatened when their spouse - whom they considered equal - starts to dominate them and leave them behind. This could occur if either spouse finds new talents, intellectual capabilities, or opportunities for advancement not available to them. Many people marry someone they see as inferior. They need to feel valued and supported by someone who respects them. This can lead to a change in the balance, as they will be able to get on better with their friends, at work, and intellectually.

One thing that seems to be happening in many marriages is the husband's ability to grow, to get promoted, expand his interests and develop new skills. His wife, however, is not encouraging him to do this.

Her job, however smart or intelligent she may appear to be, is to take care of the children. She can have her own friends but they should not be too interesting. While she may be able to join an organization and make a decent living, she should not become too obsessed with the job or work too hard. She will be encouraged, if she desires to study, to choose courses that won't be taken too seriously. And, most importantly, they must not interfere in the arrival of her dinner at his table not one minute late than the planned time.

We all need a sense that our lives are purposeful. That is why we don't often pursue it.

These are not material goals. What really matters is that each of us feels like we have done our best with the resources we have and have shared this feeling with someone who truly cares. This is a process that includes intellectual, social, emotional, as well as sexual development. Marriage is more than just an economic contract. Yet, over the years, many marriages that began with less have fallen apart until they no longer exist. Husbands and wives often need some outside help to deal with the things that have happened over the years. They also need to renegotiate contracts to give them the freedom to continue growing as individuals.

The second set of causes is often found deep inside. Each person has their own set of problems. These include worries that go back to childhood. As children, we often find temporary solutions to these problems. As adults, however we can become too busy to discover new solutions. The lonely wife is usually someone who can finally face these challenges again. This is often because her family is complete, and she is fairly secure. She might feel like there is more to the world than this. It is possible that her husband will not understand what she is talking of if she tries to get him on board.

There are no easy answers, in religion, politics or philosophy. Maybe the only choice you need to make is between accepting life as something you have never experienced and living with it.

Either you must accept it and put up with it, or you can reject it as a negative and welcome gift. You have the option to either reject it or accept it. It doesn't really matter what you think. Many people, once they accept life as their gift, discover new ways to express and develop their creative talents through poetry, music or dance. Many take the tranquillizers, leaving the matter unresolved.

All this applies to many husbands. The middle-aged man who seems to have it all is often lonely. However, on the whole, married men have a lot more opportunities than their wives to meet people and take on new challenges.

Extramarital affairs can help married couples cope with the pains of loneliness. There aren't statistics that show how many married people have an extramarital relationship. It is probably more common that most people realize. It seems that there is a conspiracy of silence regarding this subject in our society. The belief is that speaking out about the subject will encourage more people to have it, just like teenage sex. The result is that many people who find themselves in difficult situations have nowhere to turn when they need real help.

If we don't like to moralize about the events, it should be known that they can also cause great sadness and provide great joy.

Love is essential. Extra-marital affairs allow many to discover the meaning of love after having thought they'd lost it. Most affairs involve more love than sex. These are the most dangerous. There are few people who need to be reminded of the dangers involved in being unfaithful. But it is often forgotten that affairs tend to start and end in private. It can lead to feelings of loneliness, rejection, and even worsening depression if we pretend nothing has happened. People who find themselves in this type of situation are forced to look back on the good times and acknowledge that they were worthwhile. If they were.

Divorce, separation or divorce is usually the continuation of a relationship and not the cause.

Many marriages come to an abrupt end with a text or phone call.

I returned from shopping to discover this little note. It said that he was leaving me and would move to another country. I was stunned at first. I felt betrayed and angry. It felt unfair. For twenty years I had been a faithful spouse. I felt used, dirty. It turned into a woman twenty year older-she was my daughter. Later, I tried again to see him. I would have begged him on bended knees. It wasn't until three years later that my divorce was finalized that I began to see the humor in it. It was truly absurd. He didn't want or need me. But he did want me to be there. Then I realized that he didn't really love me. Looking back, I realize that we had been growing apart throughout the entire time. But I didn't know I was so lonely.

Some marriages end with a lot of drama. They split and try again. Many divorces resulted from an inability to live up to the expectations of the spouses. They often reflect adolescence more than adulthood. It might be easier to accept today's reality that while more people get married than ever, more people marry more than once. So, casualties can be expected.

But what can you do to help these people? If a woman is divorcing and has no children, or for many women who have children, one of the first lessons they learn is that husbands of married friends suddenly think they're suitable for casual affairs. One wife wrote, "After my separation, I spent the first six month avoiding my best friends who suddenly turned to gropers.

I had to give up trying to dodge them. They were never available when you actually needed them.

In divorce proceedings, both men and woman can feel some promiscuity. I consider this a healthier response than an unhealthy. This signifies a return into the marriageable state and for many people, a greater acceptance of their own worth. One of most distressing aspects of divorce trauma includes the rejection or denial of self and, in particular, the feeling that your sexual identity is not important anymore.

Worst of all are single-parents. Usually, the husband is separated, but more often the wife has young children and is divorced. Even though friends may find it consoling to say you're lucky to have kids, there are many times when you'd rather spend the money on a good man than in your bed. Of all the needs that a single parent has, sexual ones are often the least understood. Masturbation may temporarily relieve tension but it will not solve the underlying frustration that you are unable to express your sexual side by loving and sharing the body. Many people feel guilty about being sexual.

Deprived from the possibility of mutual tenderness, mutual passion, we start to devalue ourselves and succumb to the indeterminate sentence that is stage two loneliness.

This isn't an easy task. Sometimes it helps to just say you feel rundy without having to prove anything. Sometimes it's best to forget we were sexual and just put everything in cold storage. We all have different levels and desires for sex, so neither approach will work for everyone. Many will surprise themselves and decide to have sex when they are offered the chance. While it may not be the same as love and sexual intimacy, many people find it better than having no sex.

It is easy to overlook the double standards of society.

There's also the guilt.

These are all practical issues. Where can you find someone who you feel secure with, is trustworthy, who likes you, and will not make you a problem? How to save money on the bus ticket or pay the entry fee for the social gathering. How to save money for your holiday. How to find someone willing to care for the kids. What to say to the children, and so forth.

Most importantly, how to be a happy adult and fulfilled person without having your kids hurt by your mistakes.

You must be yourself. Being yourself is essential if you want to survive.

The most common stumbling block is not the somewhat casual sexual encounter, but the rush of remarrying. Do not rush to remarry. A high probability of you marrying the wrong person is the result of trying to get married on the rebound. The same goes for marrying because your friends and family believe your children need a man to live in the house. However, not because you are desperate for him, could also be a mistake. If you marry because of the shock that everyone will see, and if you don't get married, it is foolish. Marrying because you may never have another chance is foolish. Only when you are sure about the chances you are taking will you be able to make the best decisions. As you've seen, marriage doesn't guarantee your loneliness will end.

In many ways, the challenges faced by divorcing couples are very similar to those facing bereavement. Both go through mourning. A time when they feel helpless and unable to cope on their own. Both have found that people tell them to forget their worries, and to 'put everything behind you' as if it would mean they are forgetting all those important events. Both have a tendency to move away and forget all of the people, places and things they loved during their marriage.

Both may also wish to imagine the marriage in the past, but bereaved people are more likely than the others to do this as their first response. You may feel very angry at your spouse if they die in an inopportune hour and leave you to manage the affairs on your own. This is normal. Let the anger go. One of the worst things you can expect is people refusing to discuss the fact you have a deceased partner. Finding out who your real friends is the best thing. You will be able to find your true friends, and you can begin to make new friends.

The elderly can often be lonely and have poor health. This can lead the elderly to become isolated, and past misguided housing policies have only made the situation worse. Recent years have seen a greater interest in older people. Even though tragedies can often go unnoticed by large cities in these areas, it is likely that there is more being done to help those affected. There is a lack of younger people to help, especially those with the ability recognize the bright mind that is trapped in the fading.

Age doesn't mean you have a lower need for intellectual stimulation. People who find that they are more productive than ever are the ones who retire most happily. Preparing for retirement is part of the solution.

Between the middle and the end of your life, loneliness can often be a chance to reflect and review what has been happening and where you want it to go. This often leads to an ability for oneself to cope. Many people learn how to discover their own answers and reject many of the traditional values and conventions that have been handed down to them. It is not easy to be self-sufficient and happy without falling prey to guilt, shame, and selfishness. It is possible to be guilty of this, but it can also be caused by the actions of others. These attitudes, as well as the attitudes of the society, are a major factor in the devastation.

People need people

Statistics about loneliness are rarely discussed.

They are still important. It is a common fact of today's life that people don't always take social problems seriously if they are not aware of their scale. Statistics about loneliness of any type are very few.

My own research suggests that in the U.K., just over 14 per cent of people consider themselves to very lonely. Half the respondents to my study considered themselves to have been in some degree lonely. If 14 percent is projected to represent the entire population, that would mean that around one and threequarter million people believe they are lonely. That's because there are roughly twelve and half million'singles. The number of people who are married is roughly twice that of the total population. We don't know how many of them are very lonely. But it wouldn't be surprising if there weren't at least a quarter-million. Two million people could be considered.

There is no way to know the future, but two million people could be involved. It is worth asking why so little effort was made to make sure. Why is loneliness often not taken seriously. It's not recognized as a disease by more people.

One way to find out is by looking at the attitudes of people who don't feel lonely. Loneliness, which is considered a fact in life, is an occupational risk and one of the natural hazards of being a human being, is seen as something that can be expected. They suggest that if you feel lonely, it is simply a matter of luck.

There is widespread belief that the problem will not be solved.

Since there is not much that can be done, there is no reason to worry about it. Some feel sorry that victims were hurt, but others are content to know they won't be the last. Some feel less sorrow. Their belief is that loneliness is their fault.

In recent years, however there have been several campaigns in the media to raise awareness of some aspects. Unfortunately, they are often used to perpetuate misconceptions, rather that to inform, due to the fact that there is not much information. One myth is the belief that elderly people are the most lonely. My survey evidence shows otherwise. The thirties through forties are the most lonely, not the sixties and fifties. The youngest people were most lonely: the 112 respondents, aged between 15 and 20, and the sixty singles, between sixty and seventyfive and sixty five years.

These results were so remarkable that a second analysis was run to compare the 33 men who had never married with those who were single 300 women. However, the loneliness was highest among women in their fifties. Women of all ages didn't generally consider themselves lonely in any other age group. The most lonely elderly spinsters looked far and away.

Contrary to this, men saw a steady increase on loneliness throughout their twenties/thirties, peaking at forty.

Another myth similar to this is that loneliness only exists in urban areas. It's not. There were 1,000 singles who responded to my survey. Half of them lived in cities. Thirty-six percent in towns. And fourteen percent in the country. One-third of the worst affected-the seventy-22 who were the poorest among the fourteen percent)-were city dwellers. Three-quarters of them were in towns. Twenty-one percent lived in rural areas. Only forty-three% were city dwellers. They blamed the disappearance of country buses, the high cost and fuel costs of cars, as well as the lack of affordable telephones. Even if only one person is nearby, city dwellers can still find companionship, even if it's only with people who are busy. The survey revealed that not even the lowest level comfort is available for the villager, particularly to those who are divorced or have young children or may need to cope with stigma or guilt.

This is why loneliness isn't considered a condition. We must look at what people and doctors generally consider to be an illness to understand why this is.

Most people understand illness to mean something that is physical. The result of a diseased area in the body that can't be fixed or removed using medicines, pills or poultices.

This is the wrong way to treat loneliness. If you tell a doctor that you are lonely and they examine you, you are likely to be told that there is nothing wrong physically. It would not be kind to blame him.

His attitude is responsible for the entire history of Western medicine, which has done so well to prevent suffering and premature deaths. Because medical science treats the body as an independent entity from the behavior it produces it, medical science has been able make great strides.

Loneliness may be described as a behavioural disease. It is due to a person's inability or unwillingness to communicate with others.

concerned lacks the required skills. This makes it difficult for lonely people to live their lives. Parts that are connected to the behavior I call mutual behaviour with other persons cease to function. The progressive illness of loneliness is one that causes a loss in behavioural stability. This can cause a person to lose his ability to cope with life, become depressed, and then succumb to suicide despair. People who are alone cannot share because they do not have someone to share it with, or because their ability to seize any opportunities is diminished. As a result, sufferers cannot satisfy their basic human need for warmth, comforting, understanding, and the expressions of emotions. These basic needs cannot be met if the person is not in a healthy relationship. They are impossible to find, and they can be destroyed by the disease.

All of this leaves our doctors feeling extremely helpless. There is no way that they can offer all the love, support and care needed. They won't solve the problem; they will only treat symptoms.

Understanding loneliness is possible only if we understand mutual behaviours and how they affect our health. This is an entirely new concept. We aren't used to seeing the human body in medical terms. It is only half of the system which needs treatment.

Medically, we see it as a whole system. It is equally treatable and complete when it cannot produce behaviour and is anaesthetized.

Only by accepting that people need people and that their well-being depends on their ability, can we understand loneliness and provide the right treatments. It is not accepted by everyone in society that people require people. It is certainly not considered a medical need. This could partly be due to the fact that we view health as freedom from illness. Many people find the notion of positive health beyond the absence and treatment of illness difficult to grasp. It may also be because the current concepts of medicine mean that different physicians specialize in different parts.

It's easy to feel like the whole person is being overlooked. A healthy person is more than a collection of small pieces that happen to be immune to infection. Because medicine is so focused on curing symptoms, it is difficult to achieve a person who is healthy. But, one can be able to cope. Although it may not be a remarkable achievement, this does not offer the necessary philosophy to understand loneliness. Maybe this is why we are becoming more tranquillized.

It is time to examine more closely the role played in positive behaviours and why they are important.

People need one another. It has been suggested that communication plays a crucial role in each of us being able to value ourselves and our contributions to the world. The argument may be expanded upon.

The most fundamental harm loneliness does is to a person's sexuality. The sexuality of a person is not only sex. There are many expressions of sexuality. I would define sexuality to be behaviours that are derived from or support the ability of a person to relate sexually. It allows a guy to be a guy with other guys; a girl to be an adult woman with other women; men and ladies to be men together; boys to be brothers, and girls to become sisters. Both heterosexuality or homosexuality are valid forms of sexuality that are equally important.

Sexuality is directly related to the ability and willingness to relate to others as an individual in dignity, equality and freedom. As most creatures, both men and women are sexual animals from the very beginning. They can live happy and healthy lives as individuals, but they will not be able to satisfy their needs for love, understanding, and the ability to love and understand others. People need people in this way. They need them for mutual love and support as children, parents or grandparents, as well a husband, wife, or lover.

Every one of us has a different perspective on our sexuality. Each of these needs to be developed.

We communicate emotions in a way that both protects and expresses those feelings. We do not share our deepest emotions with everyone. Those of you who do, who are often seen pathetically wandering through large cities, are the ones who are most at risk. As healthy people, we keep the most vital parts of ourselves for our most intimate relationships. Without this intimacy, we risk our entire sexuality.

Deprived of intimacy, those with it find it more difficult to express feelings. Body language in normal circumstances plays a big part in intimacy and protection from outsiders. People who are isolated, or who are unable, for circumstantial reasons, to express their feelings, exhibit disturbed body languages. Investigators have found that those who are depressed show less eye contact than people who maintain normal eye contact. People who feel very alone also consider themselves to be very unattractive. People who feel lonely and are not able to communicate with others begin to think of themselves as unattractive. As a result, they develop more negative and discourageful behaviors. As each stage becomes established, communication is cut off at an increasing rate. There are fewer people who try to get to the victim. This makes him less certain that anyone can reach him.

As the individual's sexuality grows more hidden away from outsiders, it becomes increasingly difficult to access.

This can be illustrated with a case history of a very lonely person. I met Bernard, not his real name, when he turned 42. He was very difficult to converse with, but his father had died two year prior.

Bernard had joined two internet dating clubs, had tried many marriage bureaux, and had advertised in magazines for friends. At the beginning, he seemed happy and optimistic and said that he felt like able now to find a woman after his father's death.

Bernard was just eleven years old, when his mother died. He left his father to care for the boy. Bernard says this was something that should be paid for with eternal gratefulness. It was a very generous gesture by him. I could not express enough gratitude to him. Bernard was expected by his father to talk with him every evening after he came home from work.

The boy was told to just talk. Bernard was told that he had no conversation with his father if he didn't show interest. He was put to sleep and did not show any interest in his father. The boy was eventually dismissed from school and began work as a merchant. He loved it.

There was no need for him to talk much. He is now an assistant to him, although he still works for the company. None of his efforts to find a partner through the agencies have worked.

Only by looking at Bernard, you can see the traumatized nature of his body movements as he speaks to others to realize how much he has suffered from these experiences. He is humble. It is spotty, dirty and neglected. People must be willing to spend time looking at him. This is no problem to a person who is generous and kind, or someone who can afford it. However, Bernard would not be the best person to help, even though he has plenty of other people to choose from. However, his eyes are bright and can make you smile if you try to get him to laugh.

Bernard talks only with his mouth. His lack of exercise has left the muscles at his lips' corners undeveloped. There are similar muscles that remain undeveloped to the side of his eyes. An expression that is permanent is a frown which is visible above the gap between his eyebrows. He avoids eye contact and tends to keep his head still when he talks.

He does not gesture. He sits in a cramped style that is uncomfortable and seems unable move while your eyes follow him. His voice is monotonous. He uses long pauses between sentences to build formal sentences. Most people ignore the verbs or leave out the ends of sentences. Bernard.

He is oblivious to interruptions. Once you have grasped the meaning of his thought, he will continue on with great effort to end his sentence as a grammar book.

Bernard has been trying to find a wife over the last two-years. He was a faithful and grateful son, who still nursed his father until the end. I suggested that his gratitude was unnecessary. Every father would have done the exact same. It appeared that he was rehearsing his answer, as if the father who died was still speaking. 'No.

Not all fathers would do that. Fathers lead their own lives.

Bernard manages a conversation about his father but it is difficult for him to do. His work? It's fine, I suppose. Holidays?

They're not horrible. How often does he have them. About average. It is not clear where he has been. There is no one particular.

He walks with a reluctant, withdrawn shuffle when he walks. This makes it difficult to walk beside him and create strange, uncoordinated patterns with clumsiness without any impression of purpose, grace or continuity.

Bernard would like to find a wife. However, he is an inexplicably sexless individual. He seems a bit sexy and excited. Bernard's is the shop window for sexuality. His face is empty. He is devoid or feeling and yet, he cannot be the block-of-wood he seems to appear to be. Deep within the third stage, there is little left from his sexuality and, as far as anyone can tell, there's nothing left in the inside.

Bernard was severely injured in childhood and needs special attention that no one will ever provide him with until he experiences physical symptoms. His half in any communication system is so deficient in functioning apparatus, it's very difficult for him to communicate.

hard work. He takes this precaution to his own safety, since at forty-two Bernard still is a virgin. I asked him if they had ever had sex. I asked him "Have any of you ever had sexual relations?" and he almost laughed at the idea.

His reply was simple: "No!" His reply, "No!" was partially defense, as though he had accused me of doing something illegal, and partly withdrawal, informing me that if I asked such question he would end our conversation.

The truth is, sexual freedom is the main need that most of us have. To a normal, healthy adult, this involves developing a loving relationship to the other sex member, sleeping together and sharing the experiences of life. In my survey, people were asked how experienced they considered themselves to sexually.

Half of the lonely had been married. The sexual experience was the same for them as the less lonely. Seventyfive of the most severely lonely people had never been married. They were compared to the sixty eight people in the lowest loneliness group who had also never married. The stark difference in sexual experience between never-married singles and non-married singles was astounding. The most lonely were the least likely to have had any experience.

This proves the opposite of the belief that loneliness is worse if one is sexually experienced and unable find a partner. The more common argument is, "If you have never had it you are not capable of having it."

it'. In reality, the lonely are those who have not had it. Their sexuality may not be as important, because they have been in a more intimate relationship less often. Loneliness is caused primarily by lack or insufficient communication. Lack of intimate relationship value is the most damaging aspect of poor communication. One of the best antidotes against loneliness is to have a loving, sexual experience. For many, marriage is the only place where sex is allowed. This is the way they were raised. It is a common legacy of this upbringing. This makes it easy for someone to feel lonely and to reject their sexuality until they find the right one.

You don't have to be lonely to feel the sexual side of your nature. The natural and healthy nature of sexuality is part and parcel of who we are as human beings. Nobody would suggest that if you are feeling lonely, the best solution is to go and rape someone or to get in bed with someone of the opposite gender. It would be very difficult to find someone willing. It is important to recognize that sex, even if it is not a part of our love, is normal and part. The person we like the most will want to be able share the most intimate experiences in life without feeling guilty, ashamed, or dirty. Bernard made it clear in his entire presentation of himself that he rejects the most important part, which is his sexuality. This is why people need people. This is what people look for in someone special.

Meeting and Relating

Let's assume that you bought this book out of loneliness and want to make a difference. You have now learned more about loneliness, and what you can do about it. While you may have found some useful answers, you are still looking for solid advice about how you can solve your own problem.

Here is a list with some of the lonely things people have said to my in research and counseling. They are not in any order.

I don't know where to go to meet new people. There are many places that you can meet new people. Joining a group that is related to your interests is the best option. Join several groups. One shy girl joined pottery on Mondays and photography on Wednesdays. A social club was formed on Fridays. She then went rambling at weekends.

She struggled at first but was soon able to get through it. The instructors were helpful and made her feel safe. They are. If she became embarrassed, she could concentrate on the pottery / photography/rambling. She looked at her drink at the club. The most important thing for her was to be with people, and that allowed her to forget about the lonely bed-sitter.

There are many places where you can get regular information from theatres and concert halls about their upcoming shows. If all this sounds too high-brow, check out local papers for advertisements for historical pub-crawls. Although you don't need to be interested in this activity, you should be willing to give it your best shot.

I don't know the right way to start a conversation. Finding something you can do with someone is the best way to make friends. Talking to people is easier when you have something in common. You can talk at the theatre, pop concert and art gallery lecture.

I. Don't be discouraged by looking around. Don't be afraid to get going. Nobody is going to be kind enough to talk to you.

2. Never begin an opening with 'Excuse you', or a 'I'm so sorry, but'. There's no need to apologize if something has gone wrong.

3* Don't be afraid to ask for help. If you notice someone looking at something, say: "That seems interesting." I like how it looks... and can offer something equally as interesting.

4. Always smile at people's faces and don't forget about them. You don't need words to back it up. It can be used for practice, but it can also lead to a real conversation, if you're lucky.

5. Do not place pressure on others. Take the time to be happy and you will share enough with others who enjoy the same

things to make the conversation more interesting.

6. Do not try to join a happy, large group of people unless you know them.

7. Don't mistakenly think that only people looking for sex wear the most gorgeous dresses.

8. Don't go looking to have sex. If you don't have company, be happy with the company.

9. If you don't like to drink or enjoy live jazz, don't bother with pubs. It is much easier for people to talk if they have something to discuss-aside from the weather and the beer.

10. Talking about the weather should only be done when it is very dramatic. For example, a thunderstorm that knocks you out of your home with an attractive young

woman. Yesterday's weather can be just as depressing as today's news.

1. You must be careful about your timing. When you are at a film, concert or play, be sure to wait for the next interval before you start talking.

People prefer to have a conversation before, during, or after something happens. They will turn their backs on you if you force them to stop doing what is important to them. If they aren't interested, look for the transition points.

2. Be aware that strangers can be very threatening, especially when they are in large cities. If you're a stranger, it's important to clearly communicate your non-threatening position. For instance, to start with the first comment, stand sideways and turn your head.

3. You don't have to take no for an option.

4. Make sure to keep your first comment brief. If the question is not a question ask for a short answer. Questions that end in "isn't" are not acceptable. If you get the answer to a question that ends with 'isn't it?' then forget about them.

5. You should be relaxed and choose the right distance. If your contact' is standing and sitting, move further away from them than you would if both of you were standing. Otherwise, you will be talking down.

6. Do not try to sound more educated than you really are.

7. Listen with interest. Show you are interested.

8. Keep your sentences short, and make sure your voice sounds varied. Eyes can be used for both looking and as a way to discover new things. Avoid looking through your sunglasses. You can't judge if

a stranger is safe or unsafe if you don't have the ability to see their eyes.

9. Be attractive. You will be able to make someone feel attracted to you without having to convince them.

10. Remember, you'll feel better if you chat with anyone - the people who are too old, too happy or too married are great for you. They are great at chatting. If you limit your conversations to those who would make the ideal partner for you, the one-in-a-million person who will be perfect for you, it will take you a while to find that person.

Every time I have a conversation with a man, he attempts to pick me back up. Lucky you! Let one of them succeed now and then.

I can't pay for to travel. You simply can't afford to not. The street is where it's the cheapest. There are shops around, as well as places that offer tea. New York and London are full streets filled with people who want directions. Give them a map. Relax and feel the sense that there are other people around you.

Listen to them. Enjoy them. If you don't have the funds to travel, chances are you mean that you fear losing your opportunity to meet someone. You sound spoilt. Are you? Your poverty of spirit is not something you should be highlighting. Chatter is free. Don't resent it, enjoy it.

I just can't seem to meet the right kind of people. It would be easy, however, to accuse you snobbery. I suspect this is quite unfair.

It is quite normal to have high standards. In choosing friends, we all want to find people who have something in our lives. You must have someone who has something to share in order to have an engaging conversation. A similar or equivalent level of education is required most of the time.

The time. You'd be surprised at how interesting it is to hear from people once you start talking. Do you want to be right for someone?

There is another solution. While you might be trying to say that you don't meet the right kind of people, you are also trying your best to portray that you persevere despite failing. This is fascinating. What if you realized that you don't want to succeed? That you aren't sure you want to find someone you love? What are YOU trying to accomplish? To show you are trying. Whom are you trying convince? A parent who wants to take you off her hands or a husband whom you still love dearly but miss him now that he is gone? Be patient with yourself and take your time.

There's no rush. It doesn't really matter if some people you meet aren't right for you. So long as you allow them to have fun and you take the time to get to know them, you can enjoy each other. It will reduce loneliness. This will keep the fire burning until you're ready.

I'm afraid to participate. This is perfectly understandable, especially if the last time that you participated was a complete disaster.

This means you're afraid of getting hurt. However, you may have been conned by your parent into thinking that life was about not getting hurt. This is likely to have led you to be a worrier. This is because you are afraid of getting caught. While you seem confident, strong, and self-assured from the surface of your life, underneath you are as weak as a kitten. If you are involved, someone will see through your facade.

That way they may get to know your real self. I hope so. That's exactly what you want, right? Or is that it?

People turn to me when they need a shoulder. You are the one I need to cry on. It is amazing that you can be lonely when so much needs you. The answer to all your problems is right in front, right there on your shoulder. Be with them. Get involved.

They don't necessarily weep. You can just tell me their troubles. It seems as though you are disillusioned because your troubles may not be as serious as theirs. Listening to others will help you find someone better off than you.

But... Have y'all ever noticed how many people cry on your shoulder when you give them good advice? Then they come up with excuses to make themselves feel bad.

That's exactly what you are doing!

I feel sorry. You have discovered the secret to eternal youngness. There is no need to feel isolated anymore.

Tell me about it. All my friends are going to be fascinated.

It's not true that only a handful of people who spend all their time feeling sorry about themselves realize what they are doing.

I keep asking people questions, but they keep saying no. Who are these people? When I hear this one, I often recognize the signs.

On the surface, it seems like a lonely individual, usually a young male, is asking people out. Many people say "No" to all but one. But I am not being deceived these days!

I ask "Who are yelling at?". It often turns out that she is the office girl who keeps saying "No." I ask if you feel you need to address this tendency to keep doing the same thing over and over again. You are stuck, in a rut going round and round. Change is possible if you try something new. Try not to put too much effort into your life. You don't need to prove anything. I suspect that you received more attention from failing than succeeding at some point in your history. Stop making drama out of failure. Accept that you can succeed quietly and without fuss. As we learned, it can be hard to get solid advice. Most people will tell you that you're a fool, and refuse to help. Some people may give you an alibi, on condition that you never ask again. Many people will find finding it difficult to believe you can love at any age. These tips are based on years of experience counseling and interviewing people struggling with this issue.

1. Married lovers rarely break up with their spouse. They may believe they can say they will during their first affair and feel trapped. You can let go of your lover if they are caught in this trap. Give yourself permission. You must not limit it. Reduce the pressure.

2. If you are not convinced otherwise, then take all stories of the poor sex that a couple has shared with one another.

3. A married man will likely react violently if you have a second partner. He can have his wife and two-s-you, but they don't count to him as one.

4. Holidays are when your partner is with family members and you cannot be there. Do not forget to forgive your lover.

5. It is much more difficult to feel lonely when you are not able to set a date. Do not feel guilty about your engagement date.

6. It is important that you have a relationship with your partner if you are serious about having sex. This is why you should make sure that you have enough time to be with your partner and not just when he leaves. Do not try to end an intimate relationship by stopping sex or being only good friends. Do not finish.

7. If an affair ends, you'll feel alone. Also, you will be open to new relationships. Make sure you are ready. Don't succumb to the urge. Take the time to find the right key.

8. If you're able to become pregnant, do it. Abortion, adoption or raising a child on your own are all worse options than the pill and a cap.

9. If you are looking for an affair with someone who is married, or if they are in search of one, I recommend that you follow the advice of a friend: don't have a

single affair. You can only have more! It's better to avoid starting.

10. Loneliness in an affair may be the worst. The loneliness in relationships is less severe because you have the freedom to look again. And who knows what new excitement may occur. If there is too much loneliness in an affair, it could be that you are either addicted to loneliness and should quit.

RELATED TO OTHERS

Relationships do not happen overnight. They should be planned and maintained for long periods.

They take effort. You get back only a fraction of what you put in. It is possible to make some of the most common and basic mistakes in relationships. Here is more.

Communication is key to any relationship.

An earlier chapter focused on non-verbal aspects. Little was said about what and how to say it. Many readers will recognize a lot of the content. It is shocking how rarely we think of relationships. This is only a reason to be lazy or selfish.

Relationships are more damaged by greed and dishonesty than anything else. People expect too little from one another. They are more likely than others to behave like parents or equals. They can become very assertive and directive. They seek to take control of and change the person they are controlling. They do not realize that mutual behavior means accepting each other as they are.

Although you might be inclined to do so, it is quite possible that you are not aware of this. It is important to first listen to what you're saying. If you are a critical parent, then it will be easy to misuse certain words and phrases. You can try the following questions for yourself.

Do you tell people what they should or shouldn't do in certain situations? If people tell you what they are doing lately, it is not necessarily asking for you to make them right.

Do you ever tell people what they should do to solve a particular problem. If you do this, you are very close to trying and correct their behavior. You could be perceived as an authority about how they should or must run their lives. It is their life and not yours. Talking about it with them is an honor, not an invitation to take-over. It doesn't matter how intimately you know someone. You won't have any control over their life. You only have a small part of the story.

Do you want people to follow your orders? The imperative form - 'Do that!' 'Sit down!'

'Tell me!' 'Wait!' "Wait!" becomes an almost daily part of our conversation, without us even realizing. It is another indication that the bullying parent has taken control. Although these little commands may seem insignificant and innocuous, it's easy to learn the routine, especially if the bullying parent is your own. You are still telling them to behave. It just shows that you want your child to like you.

Do people make you feel annoyed or frustrated by your insistence on doing one thing? Another tactic used by bullying parents is to make people feel guilty. It's a sign you want to control someone but are becoming angry that it isn't working. Being impatient with another person is a sign you have the opportunity to learn about yourself. Sometimes, there are better ways to make use of this opportunity than hurting someone that you like.

Exercising too much, especially during the initial stages of a relationship can lead you to expect too much. Criticisms and advice are not rewardable. What types of rewards could you offer?

First, reward people who are truly interested. Flattery is not often meant with honesty. While it does not do much harm, it can quickly become tiresome. Many people already know how much attention they are worth and will soon tire of being treated in a false way. Flattery should only be used for flirting. Provided you are not simply trying to get a cheap sex, have fun with it. To be serious, and to get past the flirting phase, drop the flattery. Then be open about how you feel. Be careful, however! It is important to accept the fact that you do not want someone to be serious about you.

Second, be appropriate in giving rewards. A bouquet of red roses, a necklace with diamonds and a bracelet made from them are great gifts. But they are not the only way to impress. If they are the only reward you ever give, they will quickly lose their worth.

Sometimes, the most appropriate reward is to smile, say 'thanks', or show that you enjoy each other's company. One of the best ways to show your love for someone is to recall what they have already told you.

Thirdly, do not reward people with rewards that will bring attention back towards you. Common mistakes include saying, "That's intriguing, because last summer I did the exact same thing." Your partner may not get a look in and continue to tell you about it.

Rewards are gifts that come as a free gift, and not a payment for favors. Many a young man have invested half a week in a girl to make her sleep, only to discover that she consumes double brandy faster than him and that at the end, he's still shivering. Professionals are generally the only people who sell sex. They can save a lot of work and get more satisfaction from their jobs if they don't have to sell sex.

Exercising too much sexually during the first part of a marriage can often lead to major problems. It is common for men to assume their partner's sexual readiness without first speaking with the woman. If she isn't ready and has not been asked, it is more likely that he will get a physical rebuke than a verbal. Talk to your partner if you feel sexually attracted. Talk about it immediately, not waiting for the opportunity to present itself.

There are times when a lonely guy has sex with someone he likes, but then he loses his erection temporarily or ejaculates too early. This causes him to worry that he will not live up her expectations.

Again, the answer to this is to talk about. Sex without having a conversation is like eating without knives and forks. It's messy and not very fun. You also tend to get your fingers burnt. It helps lonely ladies to realize that they are susceptible to impotence, premature ejaculation, and other female-related issues. The worst of all is male sexual behaviour, which can result in frustration as well verbal abuse to one another's sexual prowess.

Sarcasm concerning sexual abilities is to me the ultimate obscenity.

Meeting someone's family is key to building a lasting relationship. This could mean meeting your partner's children.

They may not love you. Even more challenging is how to handle conflict between them and your partner. There are many ways to view a family conflict. But it is rare that you can play the role of the critical parent. This is sometimes the reality. You are being set up for failure. It's better to do nothing, not to get involved, and to discover as much as you possibly can about your true feelings toward your partner. If your partner is asking for your help in controlling the unruly kids of a marital breakup, it is best not to agree. You can only fail if your partner is willing to try. Your partner may need your help in resolving their emotions.

One problem with advice is its reliance on the flawed principle of if I were to you'. The second issue is that advice tends to be focused on how to cope with a problem. That is true even if you consider loneliness. A permanent solution to loneliness is necessary or you will be destroyed. A permanent cure is far better.

If you don't know how to cope, nobody can do this for or for you.

Are You a Good Person?

Coping comes second best. There are times when this is all you can manage. In such situations, you have no choice but to give up and leave nothing for your family or friends. You are able to continue to go despite not having enough. When you are coping, it is very difficult to survive.

People have to deal with many kinds of deprivation as well as fear and pain. It is often quite an inhumane process. It is possible for others to be confident that you will succeed. They will tell you that you'll be able to cope. 'You'll survive.'

They are often too confident.

They don't have to. You can. Fear and suffering are the only things that separate you. They and you will never understand one another. It is a harsh truth of life: Those who are warm don't understand the cold. Those who have never been through it can never comprehend why others who are coping do not seem to be able to. There lies the truth.

There is no dignity. There is no pride. There is no stability. If you appear to be in control, you are isolated and at your worst.

The best thing is to cope. Health is better.

Giving of your best to others.

This is just the beginning. How do you proceed with the second?

First, you need to understand why you react so strongly to loneliness. Loneliness is an effect that devalues your individual resources. How can loneliness frustrate you? What are the expectations you have for your life and what are you getting instead? Maybe your expectations are not being fulfilled. But is that really you or are they the expectations of someone else? Are they realistic goals?

All too often, we become obsessed with pleasing others.

Who are your intentions?

Second, you must recognize that loneliness can be a sign of being alone and not a sign of being isolated. To be on your feet means that you must take on responsibilities that you would prefer others to handle, but they will be overlooked unless you do. Even though it is fine to be angry and rejected, it won't help.

To be truly alone is to be human. The most important thing about each person is to be alone. Loneliness and its associated symptoms are a form of illness.

Your own self-worth is distorted first. An illness can cause you to be unable to accept other people's value and make them feel superior.

Third, be open-minded to others. Accept any sign of friendship, regardless how lonely, and make sure you return it in the same way. Some people are helped to see that they can love only themselves, and that love is possible until they accept that they are loved. Nobody, not even nobody, is invincible.

Loneliness refers to a sickness that makes you feel unlovable.

These are only a small part of the story. Loneliness has its own destructive effects because it reinforces any tendency we might have to collaborate at our own destruction.

It is a behavior disorder that leads to our behaviour becoming less survival-oriented.

But it cannot take hold if our behavior is not already self destructive. This might seem like a ridiculous idea. It is something I have witnessed many times rejected by people who drive to fast, drink too heavily, smoke too many cigarettes and work too hard. It has also been rejected by people with the look of a madman. People who do not smoke or drink, drive or work and are happy to surrender any control they had over their lives in favor of a husband who can do all of these things but cannot last forever.

This is what it means to know yourself. Understanding your self-destructive tendencies is key to understanding them. This includes learning about where they come from and how you can change them.

What IS a 'SELF DESTRUCTIVE TENDENCY'?

Each of us has one of three possible reactions when confronted with a crisis.

The flight reaction, which is the first, is when we run away. It can be expressed very well in a lapel badge that I once witnessed, which said, 'If you are unsure, panic!

There are many ways you can get rid of something. The first is the literal one. This means that we simply get out of the way. Sometimes we can run from an unpleasant situation simply by leaving the room, or by trying to ignore it, hoping it will go away.

Sometimes, running away can be the best decision. Sometimes this is easy to see. Sometimes it is clear that it is the best thing to do. Perhaps you are the kind of person who will run away when faced with a serious crisis. Or, you might be the type who is unsure if it is a good idea to run away but end up doing so. Running away decreases the value we have for those we are trying to help in a crisis. It's obvious that they may want to destroy the value of our situation. If our only function in it is to cause pain, then we should not allow them to do this.

If I flee, my value will be reduced to a hungry leopard or to a group of muggers. But if it is all that they are worth, then I'm leaving! There are many crises where my value is positive. I might be able to save myself from some of these situations, but it will cost me the long-term opportunity to be more useful.

Running away can lead to self-destructive tendencies.

We may appear to be acting in order to protect something. These things can be endangered by a crisis. To protect our value, many people run away from the crisis. But by running from the crisis, you also distance yourself from people. We diminish or destroy the value we offer these people. Runaway means we are no longer able to see the potential for what good could have been done if stayed. Running away from loneliness is the best thing for us.

The flight response is one way that we respond to crises. The fight reaction, on the other hand, is a second option. Fight can be defined as giving in to fear and fighting is the opposite. This is an acceptable response in many circumstances. If someone attempts to steal something or hurt someone we love, we will be angry and challenge their right. We are willing to fight. As with running away from home, the goal of our behavior is to keep our value or preserve the value and importance of those things or people. It is possible to give in completely to anger and act out in blind rage. Or, we may choose not to let our anger get the best of us and manage it carefully. Sometimes, we find it difficult to speak up when we are bullied, victim to emotional blackmail, or exploited. The fight reaction is a way to express your anger. Examples of fight reaction include asserting oneself and fighting for our rights.

It is evident that there are times when aggression and anger are appropriate. But anger, like fear and anxiety, is not easy to control. Some people find anger very natural. This is possible. Many things can anger and irritate your emotions. You snarl. Everything is someone else's problem. Fear does not work the same way anger does. Fear, or running away from danger, protects us by keeping us from being devalued. However, anger keeps us safe by decreasing the value of others in the situation. We maintain our position by keeping them down.

Let's look at a little puzzle. A five-pound note can be held in one hand while a one pound notes is held in the other. How can the one pound note be worth more than the five-pounder? The answer is simple: destroy the five-pound note.

It's worthless if it's torn up and burned. Anger and aggression are ways to lower the value or other people in relation to our own.

We will do everything we can to make the tiger, or the muggers, who are trying to rob and eat us, less valuable. If we succeed in fighting them, they will reduce their value enough to preserve ours.

These are obvious instances in which aggression can be helpful. But what about the more obscure cases? In any crisis involving people it is possible to hurt or put down them temporarily. If we win, they might not bother us again. Their chances of ever coming near us again are lower the more we act aggressively. We may have protected self-esteem. Pride, status. authority. Sexuality. Intellectual superiority. Savings. Integrity.

But we won't get the chance to do so again.

Some people have a need to win over others.

They are in control. They are able to put others down just to maintain their own ego. They see life as a struggle they must win. Some fight tough, while some fight fair. They are so insecure about their own value, that they will not allow it to be challenged. For them, fighting is a way to live. They are much more skilled at making others feel bad about themselves than they are at making their own feel good.

The freeze reaction is a combination of the flight and fight reactions. If you have ever witnessed a trapped bird or frightened young animal, you will have seen it freeze. Everything freezes. It is as if both the desire to run and the desire to stay and fight cancel each other out, and nothing is done.

There are many methods to freeze an individual's body. One approach is to let fight and flight have their turns, but not letting either one dominate. We may want to run away and hurt others one moment, then the other.

This is often how we experience jealousy. If we constantly see-saw from one reaction to another, we end up doing nothing. Imagine that you see-saw less violently. It doesn't matter if it is from one minute or the next but rather from one hour. This is how many people worry. Worrying is another way to freeze the brain. It's a way of not doing anything except worrying about the crisis. Even though we don't do anything about the crisis, the anger phase can cause us to regret saying things later. You may also find that you open up escape paths that you didn't plan to use during the run-away stage. Jealous lovers can be seen talking up strangers and starting new relationships. But later, they may realize they have set expectations they don't want to fulfill. People can turn to any source they want for help or advice, even if they are worried.

In some situations, the freeze reaction is appropriate. It can also be stated as: "Stop worrying about everything for a while, I want time to think." We can do no harm, but we do not make it worse. The tiger might be trying to get at someone else, or may just be seeking a friendly pat and a meal.

Two young boys might be the muggers. If we take the time to stop running away from the danger, or allowing our instinct to fight to overtake us, we might find ourselves in a dangerous situation.

However, freezing can, like fight or flight, also endanger the long-term value of the assets. It preserves only the value of the frozen items, and it may be destroyed by external events that alter them. The only thing we are able to preserve is our potential value in a situation. This is not our true value. So, when we worry, our thoughts are often filled with the words, "Perhaps if...?" or "So-and-so will probably do such-and-such." Our worrying lives are filled with many ifs. As jealous lovers, they say things like, "If only" and, "He probably thinks" or "Perhaps, she thinks..."

There are times when the three reactions to crisis: fight, flight, and freeze may all be appropriate. All three can be self-destructive.

How can they become self destructive? This behaviour is part of their animal nature. These instincts would have killed your ancestors and prevented you from ever being born. This instinct is built into you. It is up to you to manage it. That's what you must learn.

These instincts can be controlled because we have been taught. Watch any family and you will see the many different ways it is done. Children learn self-control. Part of the teaching is conscious and deliberate. Part of it is unconscious. It was learned from parents by imitation. The child is able to see when the parent loses control of their decisions or makes mistakes. The child would likely be punished if they lost control of the same manner in many families.

What most people learn in childhood, is not to feel what you show but how you act. We learn to conceal our emotions. We hide our anger, and often we don't dare to show it. If we are afraid, we conceal the fact because it would make matters worse if anybody knew. As we get better at turning anger and fear inside, it becomes easier to let go of the fear. Instead of being upset with others, we can be angry with ourselves. Instead of feeling fear, we flee from a portion of ourselves. Because there is no other way, we internalize conflict. We internalize the conflict because our instinctive reaction to external trouble is to bring it in. Sometimes, it is possible to manage the problem from within. Often we cannot. Some people live alone and have trouble storing their problems, which no one wants to know.

These self destructive tendencies are self-preservation and self-preservation gone wrong. Loneliness can grip us. Everything we do becomes questionable if it isn't loved enough. For each person to live through childhood and to grow up, they must feel loved. Anger with people is not a way to make them love you. And if we fear them, they won't love us. We can't show our anger or fear. The sad thing is that even though we cannot express our anger or fear, this does not make it go away. We can fight it. All these things are possible. But if you are lonely, all these things can be done alone.

There is only a single answer to all these questions. The answer is love. People who aren't lonely aren't those who have no fear or anger. They fight, run away, freeze, and they fight. They love despite the fear. They love despite the anger.

They allow love to free them from their frozen bodies when they need it. Love is the only way people can set a permanent price for their lives. Love values what they are, but not what they do. We won't feel the joy of love and being loved if we don't try to be loved because of what we do.

Coping is second only because it restricts the love we feel for others, and limits the expression of that affection.

People love to be controlled. We see people who aren't afraid to give and take no for granted. They are managing.

Is this all that you want to do? Or do you dare to risk being loved because of who you are, not what your do? Is it possible to treat others in the same manner you would want to be treated?

Every person has the instinct to defend their own lives, to keep the will to live, to make a contribution to the survival and well-being of all life. We cannot do all this by ourselves. If we keep our thoughts and experience to ourselves, our knowledge and skills will all die. If we share just a bit of all this, the rest will live on somewhere else, even for a limited time.

We have a fear of giving away our own control. We can't give and receive if you don't.

And who else are we to give away than ourselves?

WEEK 1

Day 1

Jeremiah 29:13 (NASB)

'You will search Me and find Him when you search for me with all your heart.

Day 2

John 14 (NIV)

"Don't allow your heart to become troubled. Trust God, trust also in Me

Day 3

Deuteronomy 4:31 (NASB)

"For God is compassionate, LORD."

He will not fail to you or destroy your fathers, nor forget the covenant that He made with them."

Day 4

Psalm 27:10 (NASB)

My father and my mom have forsaken both me.

But the LORD is my strength.

Day 5

John 14;6 (NIV).

Jesus answered, "I'm the truth and my life.

Only I can bring you to the Father.

Day 6

Isaiah 41:10 (NASB)

"Do Not Fear, I am with YOU!"

Day 7

John 16.32 (NIV).

My Father is with us, so I am not by myself.

WEEK 2

Day 8

Joshua 1:5 (NASB)

"No man will be in a position to stand before or serve you throughout your entire life.

As Moses was with me, so I am with you.

I will always be there to support you.

Day 9

Psalm 38:9 (NASB)

All that I desire, Lord, is Yours.

And You can see that I am sighing.

Day 10

Psalm 147:3 (NASB)

He heals brokenhearted

And it binds them up.

Day 11

Deuteronomy 31:6 (NASB)

"Moreover, The LORD your God is going to circumcise your heart as well as the hearts of your descendents.

To love the LORD with all your heart, soul and soul.

so you may live.

Day 12

Genesis 2:18 (NASB)

The LORD God answered, "It does not make sense for man to be all alone;

I will make him the best helper for him."

Day 13

Psalm 23:4 (NASB)

Even though I am walking through the valley under the shadows,

I am safe because You are there for me.

Your rod and Your staff are comforting me.

Day 14

Romans 8:31 (NASB)

If God is with us, who's against us?

WEEK 3

Day 15

Psalm 139:1-2 (NASB)

O LORD, you have searched me.

You know when i sit down and when i rise up.

From afar, you can understand my thought.

Day 16

Proverbs 15:13-14 (NASB)

A happy heart can make a cheerful face.

When the heart feels sad, the spirit can be broken.

Day 17

Hebrews 13:5-6 (NASB)

Be content in what you have

He Himself spoke,

"I Will Never Desist You, And I Will Never Forsake You."

So that we can confidently say:

"THE LORD is MY HELPER.

WHAT WILL THE MAN DO TOME?"

Day 18

Isaiah 51:11 (NASB)

The LORD's ransomed will be returned.

You are invited to Zion with joyful shouting

And they will live in everlasting joy.

They will be filled with joy and gladness.

Sorrow and sighing will go away.

Day 19

1 Peter 5-6 (NIV).

You must humble yourself, to be under God's mighty hand.

He will lift you up at the right time.

All your anxiety can be put on him as he is there for you.

Day 20

Hebrews 10-24-25 NIV

Let's consider how to encourage one another towards love and good works.

Do not let us forget to meet up together.

As some are habitual of doing

We can all be encouraged as we watch the Day approach.

Day 21

Galatians 5:25 (NIV)

Keep in step with Spirit since we live by Spirit.

WEEK 4

Day 22

1 Timothy 5:5 (NIV)

The widow who is truly in desperate need of help, and has been left all alone, puts her trust in God

It is a habit that continues throughout the night to pray and ask God for assistance.

Day 23

Hebrews 4:15-16 NIV

We don't have high priests who are unable to understand our weaknesses.

But, there's one who's been tempted in every possible way.

Just as you are - but was not without sin.

Let us then approach with confidence the throne that is grace.

For mercy and grace to be shown to us when we need it most.

Day 24

Galatians 5:22-23 (NIV)

But the fruit and gift of the Spirit are love, joys, peaces, patiences kindnesses, goodness, faithfulness to the Lord, gentleness, and self-control.

Day 25

2 Timothy 3:16-17 (NIV)

All Scriptures have been given by God and are useful for teaching, rebuking, and correcting

Training in righteousness

so that God's man might be fully prepared for every good task.

Day 26

John 14:14 - NIV

I will answer any question you might have about me.

Day 27

Psalm 142:5-7 (NASB)

"I cry to O LORD; I tell you, "You have my refuge, my share in the land of living."

Listen to my cries. I need your help.

Give me liberty from my prison to praise your name.

Then all the righteous people will gather about me because I am good to them.

Day 28

James 4-8 (NIV).

God will draw you nearer if you are willing to be his guest.

WEEK 5.

Day 29

Isaiah 40:11 (NASB)

Like a shepherd, He will take care of His flock.

He will gather His lambs.

Take them with you in His bosom

He will lead the nursing sheep gently.

Day 30

Psalm 25:16-17 (NASB)

"Turn to Me and Be Grateful to Me,

Because I am lonely and suffering.

Troubles of the heart are getting bigger

Take me out!

www.ingramcontent.com/pod-product-compliance
Lightning Source LLC
Chambersburg PA
CBHW050405120526
44590CB00015B/1838